The Dog Who Saved Halloween

Allan Zullo

Scholastic Inc.

To my youngest grandchildren, Jack Manausa and Ella and Dash Gorospe, with hopes they will always possess the fun spirit of Halloween.

—A.Z.

Photos ©: cover: ktmoffitt/iStockphoto; bats background throughout: Vector Patterns; icons throughout: arose373/iStockphoto.

ISBN 978-0-545-76975-4

10 9 8 7 6 5 4 3 2 1   16 17 18 19 20

Printed in the U.S.A.   40

First printing 2016

Book design by Lizzy Yoder

Contents

Pawesome Pets   1

The Dog Who Saved Halloween   3

The Runaway Horse   23

The Ghost Cat of Edgewater Towers   42

The *Lechuza*   62

The Witch's Cat   81

The Love Bird   102

The Cemetery Dog   122

Pawesome Pets

Don't you just love Halloween? Dressing up in funny, clever, or scary costumes. Trick-or-treating through the neighborhood. Stuffing yourself with candy and other goodies.

But kids aren't the only ones who make Halloween special. Pets do, too. About 13 percent of American adults dress up their pets in costumes, spending about $350 million a year, according to the National Retail Federation. It makes sense. Pets are part of families' everyday lives, so why wouldn't Fido and Fluffy take part in Halloween?

Millions of people take their costumed pets trick-or-treating, dress them up to greet visitors at the door, or bring them to Halloween parties. Whether the family dog looks like a four-legged Darth Vader or the family cat is a pint-sized, furry version of Harry Potter, it's all in good fun.

In the following pages, you will read stories of dogs, cats, birds, and a horse who turned Halloween into a holiday to remember. The stories are loosely based on, or inspired by, true-life events, although dialogue has been added and scenes have been dramatized. In many cases, names have been changed.

Some of the accounts in this book spotlight the mischievous and naughty side of the animal kingdom. Other stories feature heartwarming moments that illustrate the animals' loving and devoted natures. All of these tales are reminders of how these remarkable creatures have helped make Halloween one of the most enjoyable times of the year.

The Dog Who Saved Halloween

The abandoned two-story farmhouse was spookier than Leo Cooke had imagined it would be. The late-afternoon autumn sun cast the gloomy place in a reddish glow, prompting him to tell his girlfriend, Miranda Sykes, "The house looks like it's blood-stained."

She punched him in the arm and said, "Oh, stop it. You're just trying to scare me."

Shadows from the swaying bare trees pranced against the weathered wood siding. "See?" he said. "Don't the shadows remind you of dancing skeletons?"

"Will you cut it out, please?" said Holly Haynes. She squeezed the hand of her boyfriend Adam Rocha, Leo's best friend and teammate on Auburn High School's wrestling squad.

Vines that had grown unchecked for years had snaked their way up the exterior walls and into several broken windows, including ones on the second floor. Bluish-green moss spread out along the slanted roof of the sagging front porch like a moldy blanket.

"Yep, this is the place all right," said Adam. "This is where Old Man Anson was killed. So, is everyone ready to go inside?"

Although Leo had some misgivings, he wasn't going to show any fear in front of his friends. "Sure, yeah, let's do it—unless you all are too scared," he said.

"We're here to photograph the ghost, so let's do it," said Miranda, trying to act bold.

Leo pet the head of his yellow Labrador retriever, Sandy. She was following a few steps behind the foursome, who were stomping through the waist-high weeds of the overgrown field that fronted the house. *I'm glad I brought her along,* Leo thought.

According to the local legend, this deserted house off Country Road 109 had been haunted for the past sixty years—ever since farmer Duncan Anson had been murdered there. Leo had researched the *Register-Times* newspaper to confirm that farmhand Gerald Morris had killed Anson. Testimony during the murder trial revealed that Anson had accused Morris of stealing and selling two of the farmer's cows. Morris denied it, but was fired anyway. After Anson convinced his fellow farmers not to hire Morris, the farmhand became so incensed he stormed into the house and killed his former employer. Morris was convicted of first-degree murder.

Over the years, people reported seeing Anson's ghost peering out of the window. Passers-by claimed they heard loud, eerie moans coming from inside. Because today was Halloween, it seemed like the perfect time to discover if the house was truly haunted—and, if so, gather photographic evidence of Anson's ghost.

As the foursome approached the ramshackle house, Sandy's tail was down. It was obvious from her body language that she was not thrilled to be here.

"Am I the only one creeped out?" asked Holly.

The door was boarded up, but the front windows had been removed years earlier. "Who's going to climb in first?" asked Miranda. "Because I'm not."

"Rock paper scissors?" Adam asked Leo.

Leo agreed. He lost. He stepped through the open window and then called, "Come on, Sandy." She hesitated, but being an obedient dog, she jumped into the room, a dusty parlor. The others followed.

There wasn't much to see. The place was empty of all furniture. However, the walls of peeling plaster displayed several decades' worth of graffiti that had been scrawled with spray paint or carved with penknives. Among them: DEATH TO ALL WHO ENTER and LEAVE!!!

Suddenly, they heard a strange yowling sound coming from another part of the house. It lasted only for a second or two. "Did you hear that?" Miranda asked.

"You don't think it's Old Man Anson, do you?" Adam said mockingly.

"Quit trying to scare us," said Holly.

Sandy growled. "What is it, girl?" Leo said. The dog slowly prowled toward the hallway with Leo right behind her. "There's that yowl again." When they entered the hallway, Sandy jerked back in surprise. "Whoa!" shouted Leo. "What was that?"

"What was what?" Holly asked, edging away from the others and closer to the open window.

"Some small animals streaked across the hallway and into another room. It's too dark in here to tell for sure what they were."

With Sandy by his side, Leo entered the room and saw that the animals had escaped out an open window. Then he froze. "Oh, geez, you have to see this," he called out to the others. When they came in, they gasped. Leaning upright against the opposite wall was an old six-sided wooden coffin.

Before anyone spoke another word, the coffin lid swung open, revealing a human skeleton, which lunged forward before falling on its face. Sandy was the first to flee, followed by Holly, who was shrieking in panic, then Miranda, who was screaming so loudly her throat hurt, and Leo, who had never been so scared in his life. They ran out of the room, leaped out the parlor window, jumped off the porch, and ran until they felt safe enough to turn around.

When they did, they saw Adam standing on the porch, hands on his knees, laughing so hard he couldn't breathe. When he finally stopped roaring, he pointed to them and said, "Oh, did I prank you! If only you could have seen the looks on your faces. Sheer terror!"

"I hate you, Adam Rocha!" Holly yelled.

Leo was irked at Adam but also relieved that it wasn't a real-life supernatural encounter. And, reluctantly, he felt Adam deserved some props for pulling off the prank.

"I set it up with wires and pulleys earlier today," Adam confessed as he wiped away his tears of laughter. "Come here. I'll show you."

Just as they entered the house again, they heard a loud bang coming from the coffin room. "Okay, time for me to exit, guys," said Holly.

The other three and Sandy crept into the room and saw that a cabinet which had been on the wall had mysteriously fallen to the floor. "It's probably my fault," said Adam. "I drilled some holes to screw in the pulleys and must have weakened the cabinet." He put the fake plastic skeleton into the coffin and closed the lid. "My brother is coming later tonight with a bunch of friends. I can't wait to scare them."

They headed back into the parlor when Sandy, who had remained in the coffin room, began barking. Leo returned to the room and saw that the dog was sniffing and pawing at the fallen cabinet. Her bark had turned into a whine. "What's going on, girl?" he asked. Then he heard a slight mewing sound coming from under the cabinet.

He lifted it up and jumped back in surprise when a kitten scooted out. Sandy chased the cat and cornered it, but made no other threatening moves even though the hissing kitten swiped at the dog's nose.

Leo took off his jacket and wrapped the kitten in it. "Look what I have," Leo said to his friends. Stepping out onto the porch where it was lighter, Leo got his first good look at the young male cat, whose green eyes revealed more fright than feistiness. His shorthair coat was covered in a random series of light- and dark-orange swirls. "He's an orange tabby," Leo announced.

"It looks like his fur was tie-dyed," said Miranda. "Isn't he just the cutest thing?"

Pointing to the cat's forehead, Leo said, "See? This guy carries the tabby signature M marking above his eyes, only his looks more like an H."

"How is it that you know so much about cats?" Holly asked.

"I used to volunteer at an animal shelter," Leo said.

"The cabinet must have fallen on the poor kitten, but it didn't crush him because it didn't have a back," said Miranda. "By landing right-side up, the cabinet trapped him."

"If Sandy hadn't alerted us, this little fellow would have died," said Leo, rubbing the kitty's head. "He's a stray. The animals I saw running across the hallway were likely the mama cat and her kittens. Who knows if they'll return. He looks about three months old and fairly healthy, so he probably could survive on his own."

"Leo," said Miranda, "you can't leave him here alone."

So that's how Leo Cooke and his family ended up with a new member of the household. They called the cat Halloween. No other name was even considered. "We found him on Halloween, he's the color of Halloween, and he has an *H* on his forehead for Halloween," Leo told the family. "The name is a no-brainer."

While Sandy tended to favor Leo over his younger siblings—Luke, nine, and Lucy, eight—Halloween was clearly Lucy's cat. He slept with her, usually on top of her pillow, and curled up in her lap whenever she read or watched TV. But his good buddy was Sandy, who five years earlier had been a stray herself.

Back then, the children's elderly great-aunt, Rose Endicott, was a volunteer for the local animal rescue shelter where Leo also helped out for a school service project. Early one morning, Rose arrived to open the shelter and was startled to see that during the night someone had chained a one-year-old female yellow Labrador to the front door. The dog was in bad shape, skinny and stunted, due partly to an awful tapeworm infection. But despite her condition, she was upbeat and friendly.

Rose brought the dog, whom she named Sandy, back to her home where she fostered a dozen cats while they waited for new owners. She also fostered two other dogs at the time. The canines stayed in the basement, where they had access to the yard through a doggy door. Cats ruled a large room on the main floor. That way, there was no chance the dogs and cats would come face-to-face, or, more likely, fang-to-claw.

Although Sandy was an easygoing dog, no one seemed to want her. She had been adopted out but then abandoned a second time, so Rose took her in again. Rose noticed that every time Sandy went past the door leading to the cat room, the dog would paw at it. "No, you can't go in there," Rose would tell her. Sandy looked so sad that finally Rose gave in.

Clutching the leash, Rose led Sandy into the cat room. Some of the cats puffed up and arched their backs. Others froze, and then stalked, stiff-legged, slowly around the perimeter with indignation. The rest scrambled to the highest spot they could reach. But unlike most dogs, Sandy didn't harass them. Over time, she gained the trust of many—but not all—of the cats. Soon she became a member of the cat-care team, following Rose and her pet-sitters as they fed and played with the foster felines.

One day, one of the kittens slipped out of the room and dashed into the hallway with Sandy in hot pursuit.

The dog cornered the kitten and then gently kept it from fleeing. After that, any time a foster cat escaped, Sandy would herd it back inside. If she couldn't get the cat to return, she would block it, then stand and wait for Rose.

Rose had no idea why Sandy had this love and concern for cats because the dog seemed to act against her basic instincts. "I guess Sandy wanted a home so badly that she would do anything—even herd cats—to prove that she belonged," Rose once told the family. Whatever the reason, the dog's efforts paid off. Rose stopped looking for a new owner for Sandy and adopted the dog herself.

But a year later, Rose died of old age. By then, the cats and dogs had been placed in homes, and Sandy came to live with the Cookes. Leo, then eleven, and the dog formed a close bond that grew stronger over the years.

Now in high school, Leo wasn't home as much because of wrestling practice and other extracurricular activities. Sandy didn't seem to mind because she spent time with Halloween the cat. The two of them often napped together in the Cookes' sunroom. Occasionally, when they were really energetic, they chased each other throughout the house. But when Lucy was home, Halloween was devoted to her.

As loving as Halloween was, he was a scaredy-cat. Any loud noise, any sudden movement, any stranger would frighten him. He would scamper under the couch or into the next room and hide. He wanted to stay indoors—especially after what happened to him about four months after he arrived at the Cooke household.

Miranda had come over to help Leo baby-sit Luke and Lucy on a Saturday afternoon. After playing outside, the little kids came in and convinced Miranda and Leo to play a board game with them.

Luke dragged out a step stool and went into the closet that stored games. While reaching for the Yahtzee box, he accidentally jostled a large plastic container of art supplies on the shelf. It toppled on his head, causing him to lose his balance. Luke fell off the step stool as he, the container, and several board games crashed to the floor. Fortunately, he wasn't hurt, although he did exaggerate a limp, garnering much sympathy from Miranda and Sandy, who licked his hand.

About ten minutes into the game, the dog went over to Leo and began to whine. "What is it, girl? Are you hungry?" he asked. She started walking toward the back door, then turned around and barked.

"Oh, you want to go out." He followed her into the kitchen, where he noticed the back door had been left slightly ajar. "Those kids forgot to shut the door. But you could have gone out on your own. Why did you need me?"

Sandy then bolted outside and raced over to a tall pine tree in the backyard. Circling the tree was the neighbor's dog, Bart. He was a Basenji—a tan-and-white, mid-sized, shorthaired hunting dog who doesn't bark. Bart and Sandy didn't get along, so when Bart saw her, he took off through the bushes and into his own yard. Sandy stopped at the tree.

Figuring that all Sandy wanted was to run off Bart, Leo closed the door and returned to the family room. No one was at the table. "Where is everyone?" Leo hollered.

"We're looking for Halloween," Miranda called out from Lucy's bedroom. "We can't find him anywhere."

While they searched the house, they kept hearing Sandy. Her barks sounded more frantic than the typical get-out-of-my-yard variety. Leo went outside and saw Sandy under the pine tree, looking up at something. She was known to chase a squirrel or two up a tree, but she never carried on quite like this.

"What do you see, girl?" he asked. Staring up at the pine tree, Leo slowly walked around the trunk until he spotted something small and orange-like about halfway up the thirty-foot pine. "Tell me it isn't Halloween," he muttered to himself. He looked again from another vantage point. "Oh, geez, it is."

From the open back door, Miranda said, "We still can't find Halloween."

"I know," Leo replied. Pointing to the tree, he said, "That's because he's up there."

Moments later, Leo was dealing with a little sister who was crying and a little brother who was laughing. And Sandy was alternating between whining and barking. Finally, when everyone calmed down, Miranda asked Leo, "So what are you going to do?"

"I guess I'll climb the tree and bring him down."

"It's too dangerous. Just leave him alone. He'll come down on his own. All cats do. You've never heard of someone finding a cat skeleton in a tree."

Leo shook his head. "Cats are not squirrels. Cats are great climbers, but they're not good at coming down. The only way they can work their way down is by going backward, and most cats don't know how."

Between sobs, Lucy begged, "Please, Leo, save my kitty. Save Halloween!"

Miranda bent down and hugged Lucy. Turning to Leo, Miranda asked, "Should we call the fire department?"

"Nope," Leo replied. "They only deal with real emergencies. I'll have to get Halloween myself."

He went into the garage and brought out an extension ladder and set it against the tree. He tossed a backpack over his shoulder, slipped on a pair of work gloves, and said, "Wish me luck."

After climbing fifteen feet, Leo stepped off the ladder and onto one of the tree's many sturdy branches. As he inched his way closer, he talked soothingly to Halloween, who was bunched up like a ball, clutching a branch, and shaking like a wind-tossed pinecone. Leo could tell the cat was freaked out. With green eyes as big as marbles, Halloween began a low growl that slowly rose in pitch—the classic feline sound of fear.

"It's okay, kitty," he said softly. "I've come to help you." He was now almost within reaching distance. Halloween looked up as if to contemplate whether he should climb higher. "Sweet kitty. Easy, easy." Leo slipped off the backpack and opened it. The cat looked at Leo and then at the branch above. *It's now or never*, thought Leo. With his left arm gripping the tree trunk, Leo shot out his right hand and clutched the cat by the back of the neck. "I got him!" Leo shouted down. Halloween, who was out of his mind, let out a fierce yowl and flailed away with his claws, trying to swipe at Leo's wrist. In one quick motion, Leo stuffed the cat into the backpack and zipped it up.

While the cat was snarling, yowling, and scratching inside the backpack, Leo carefully worked his way to the ground. Sandy barked her approval at the rescue, wagged her tail, and sniffed at the backpack, which moved crazily as the berserk cat tried tearing his way out. Leo brought Halloween into the house, went into Lucy's bedroom, and let him out of the backpack. The cat scurried under the bed and stayed there. After leaving a bowl of water and a few cat treats, Leo closed the door and told the others, "Let's give him time to settle down."

Back in the family room, Leo said, "I think I know what happened. The kids left the back door open. Halloween was walking by the closet when Luke and the games fell to the floor. That spooked the cat, and he flew out of the open door and into the backyard. Then Bart showed up and chased him up the tree. Basenjis can't bark so we weren't alerted to Halloween's predicament—but Sandy knew. She was barking to let me know that Halloween was in trouble. By the way, where is Sandy?"

Miranda said, "Look down the hallway."

There was Sandy lying on her belly in front of Lucy's door, waiting for her buddy to get over his traumatic ordeal.

When the next Halloween (the holiday) rolled around eight months later, the family knew Halloween (the cat) needed to be kept away from the front door and trick-or-treaters. The Cookes locked him in Lucy's room to avoid another crisis. While Mrs. Cooke stayed home to hand out candy, Mr. Cooke and Sandy went out with Lucy and Luke, who were dressed in matching red-and-black ninja warrior outfits complete with plastic swords that lit up.

That same night, Leo and Miranda, along with Leo's pal Adam and Laura Rogers, who was Adam's latest girlfriend, had driven into the country to explore an old barn that was allegedly haunted. They met up with several of their classmates, but nothing much happened. Well, there was one moment that petrified them. Caught in the beam of Adam's flashlight, a wraith—a ghastly old woman in tattered garb—flew down from the rafters, scattering the young people, who screamed and hollered in alarm. When they recovered from their fright, they found Adam doubled over with laughter. Earlier in the day, he had rigged the fake ghost to a wire and set it on a rafter. Then, at the appropriate time, the prankster pulled on a second wire that released the ghost so it could swoop down on the group.

The night ended early when the owner of the barn showed up and shooed everyone out, so the two couples drove to Leo's house with a plan to raid Lucy's and Luke's candy haul. Having returned from trick-or-treating a few minutes earlier, Lucy, who was still in her ninja costume, went into her bedroom, scooped up Halloween, and headed for the living room to play with him. "This is the best Halloween ever," she told him.

When Lucy was crossing the foyer, Adam—wearing a realistic teenage werewolf mask—burst through the front door, planning to scare Mrs. Cooke. Instead, he terrified Lucy—and Halloween. The girl screamed in horror. The cat yowled and flew out of her arms. He whooshed past Adam, sailed out the door, ran between Leo's legs, rocketed past Miranda and Laura, and bounded into the darkness.

Adam ripped off his mask, dropped to his knees in front of the wailing Lucy, and tried to apologize. "Oh, Lucy, I'm so, so sorry," he said. "No need to cry. It's me, Adam. I was trying to play a joke on your mommy. I didn't mean to scare you."

Meanwhile, Leo had spun around, shouting, "Halloween! Come back! Come back!" He and his friends ran after the crazed cat, but in the night it was impossible to see where he went. They returned to the house where the distraught girl cried out in anguish, "My cat is gone, and he's never coming back! This is the worst Halloween ever!"

Leo grabbed several flashlights and passed them out to his friends. "Where's Sandy?" he asked his father.

Mr. Cooke replied, "I let her out the back just a few minutes ago."

Leo went into the backyard and called for Sandy, but she wasn't within earshot. *Oh, great,* he thought. *Now we have both pets missing.*

He went inside and told the others, "Let's spread out and cover the neighborhood. Keep calling for Sandy. She must have heard the commotion and sensed that the cat was in trouble. I have a feeling that if we find Sandy, we'll find Halloween."

Leo and Miranda had walked about a block, calling out the dog's name, when Miranda said, "Look! The corner up ahead!"

Leo caught a glimpse of Bart sprinting under the glow of the streetlight on Roberts Avenue. Sandy, about fifty feet behind, was running after him. "Do you think they're chasing after Halloween?" Miranda asked.

"Probably," said Leo. "Come on, let's follow them."

Miranda, who starred on Auburn High's cross-country and track teams, took off like a shot. Leo, the conference's top wrestler in the 152-pound weight class, couldn't catch up to her.

Two blocks away, Roberts Avenue dead-ended at a wooden pier that jutted out into a large pond. As Leo neared the pier, he heard Sandy bark madly and Miranda scream, "Oh, no!"

When Leo arrived, Miranda was waving her flashlight back and forth, aiming it at the water. Bart was panting heavily off to one side of the pier while Sandy was yelping from its front edge. She was on her stomach with her front paws dangling over the side.

Keeping her eyes glued on the water, Miranda was all choked up, but managed to blurt out, "Oh, Leo, this is awful! I saw Halloween run down the pier and disappear. He must have flown off into the water, but I don't see . . ."

She stopped when she heard a splash. Sandy had leaped into the water and was now paddling away from the pier. Leo and Miranda kept their flashlights trained on the dog until seconds later the beams shined on Halloween, who was struggling to stay afloat. As Sandy reached his side, the panicky cat immediately climbed onto her back. Sandy then turned around and, with Halloween hanging on, paddled to the pond's bank where Leo seized Halloween and lifted him off the dog.

"I've got you, kitty," he said softly. "You're safe now." The cat was so frightened that he couldn't do anything but shiver. Leo gently placed him inside his jacket to keep him warm and confined.

Sandy trotted out of the pond and growled at Bart, who was sitting on the pier, panting and acting like nothing had happened. After shaking water off her coat, Sandy went over to Leo, and looked at him as if wondering where Halloween was. Leo unzipped his jacket just enough to show that her soaking-wet buddy was okay.

"Sandy, you are awesome," Leo declared. "You're a lifesaver."

When they returned to the house with the two soggy animals, Lucy began crying again—but this time out of happiness. After smothering her cat with kisses, she announced, "It was the best Halloween and then it was the worst, and now it's the best again."

"We have Sandy to thank for that," said Leo, bending down to hug his dog. "She saved Halloween—in more ways than one."

The Runaway Horse

Annabelle Squires desperately wanted to win the Southcliff Equestrian Center's horse-and-rider Halloween contest, especially after finishing second the previous year to her best friend and sixth-grade classmate, Brooke Logan.

Everyone agreed that Brooke had deserved the orange-and-black first-place ribbon. She had dressed her mare, Nutmeg, in a scarecrow costume with burlap pants stuffed with straw on the horse's front legs, and a straw hat with holes cut out for the ears. Cornstalks were woven around her saddle, and a large checkered kerchief hung around her neck. Brooke sat atop the horsey scarecrow in a blackbird costume—complete with wings—that her parents had bought online.

Annabelle didn't stand a chance. Using fake fur from a craft store, she turned her quarter horse, Blaze, into an oversized poodle with poofs on his legs and tail, and a wig with furry ears on top of his head. The girl was dressed in a pink 1950s poodle skirt, pink sweater, black-and-white saddle shoes, and a wig with a pink bow.

Although she and Brooke were BFFs, they were also competitors at most everything. No matter the contest, Annabelle always seemed to come in second behind Brooke. On a recent math test, Brooke earned a 100, Annabelle 96. In the 4-H Youth Development intermediate division archery contest, Brooke topped Annabelle 684–672. In the latest barrel race, Brooke beat out Annabelle by three-tenths of a second.

For the Halloween contest, the two girls agreed not to tell each other in advance how they were going to dress up their horses or what costumes they were going to wear. They would see each other's getup at the Equestrian Center.

Annabelle had been around horses all of her life. In fact, she had been horseback riding on her mother's lap even before she could walk. That's because her parents, Norm and Julie, owned Flying Cloud Stables, so grooming, riding, and training horses were in the girl's blood. She loved horses and they loved her.

For this year's Halloween contest, Annabelle decided to ride a different horse than Blaze. She had formed a strong attachment to a gelding called Boomerang—a dark-brown part-Arabian, part-quarter horse. The girl planned to go as an equestrian British punk rocker because it was a look that hadn't been done before, and she loved the music of The Clash and Billy Idol (as well as the American-born Ramones).

Boomerang had come into Annabelle's life months earlier. Her parents had received a call from Simone Holland, a friend who said she knew of a six-year-old gelding that needed a home. He had been a ranch horse who had outlived his usefulness. His owner didn't believe in adopting out, or re-homing, his horses after he was through with them. Instead, he sent them to a feedlot with instructions that they go straight to the slaughterhouse.

"This horse was kept in a holding pen for a week with other horses," Simone explained. "Some were waiting to go to new homes, and some, like him, were waiting for a truck to take them to a kill house in Canada.

"This horse was determined not to end up in a glue factory or as dog food. He unlocked the gate in the feedlot holding pen. And then, believe it or not, he loaded himself into an open trailer with other horses that were going to be re-homed. But the workhands saw what he had done, so they took him out and put him back in the pen with the doomed horses.

"Wouldn't you know that the next time they were loading up horses for adoption, the very same gelding unlocked the gate and went right into that horse trailer? Once again, they got him out and returned him to the holding pen.

"Incredibly, that gelding unlocked himself again and joined horses bound for re-homing. Well, the third time was the charm. The feedlot attendant told the trailer owner, 'Just take him. He's a nice boy and very smart. He deserves a chance at a life.' So will you take him?"

"After hearing this story," Julie told Simone, "how could we possibly turn him away?"

The horse was fairly healthy although he suffered from hoof problems. But a few visits from the farrier (a specialist in the care of a horse's hooves) took care of that. The horse wasn't big, standing 14.2 hands tall (the equestrian measurement for fifty-eight inches from the ground to the base of his neck), but he had a muscular build and a sleek, dark bay coat. He had a handsome face but his wild eyes gave the appearance that he was always tense and nervous, which he was most of the time. However, Boomerang had a good disposition and a willing attitude.

The horse's original name was Boomer, but Annabelle changed it to Boomerang because of the three times he came back from facing certain death. He and Annabelle hit it off from the start. She enjoyed spending time with the horse, feeding, grooming, and riding him. Sometimes she sat out in the grass while he grazed nearby. She talked to him about school and horses and her growing interest in boys—well, at least one who was a calf roper. She also sang to Boomerang.

"If you open up to a horse, and let him get to know and trust you, you'll form a strong bond," Annabelle's mom told her. "It's obvious you're important to Boomerang because when you go out into the field, he usually stops what he's doing, leaves his buddies, and walks over to you on his own."

Most days after school and on weekends, Annabelle would saddle Boomerang and take him out for a ride. The ranch was situated on a gravel road lined with houses on multi-acre lots where kids played, dogs barked, and people mowed lawns on tractors. The road saw its fair share of dirt bikes, all-terrain vehicles (ATV), and pickups. To reach some of the horse trails, Boomerang had to trot along the road, so it was a good place for him to learn to deal with the noise and distractions.

Whenever Boomerang started acting jittery and his ears began to twitch, the girl knew exactly how to calm him down. "Take it easy, boy," she cooed in a soft, gentle voice. "Everything is going to be just fine. That's right, Boomerang, stay cool. No problems."

After several months, the horse became less frazzled. Annabelle figured her rides with him had finally desensitized him to sudden noises. She was wrong.

One day, she was on Boomerang along the road when a kid on an ATV roared out from a blind lane about twenty yards in front of them. Annabelle felt Boomerang's body tense up. She leaned over to pat him on the neck and said, "It's okay, boy. Easy does it."

If Boomerang heard her, he paid no attention. Instead, he panicked and took off on a dead run. He galloped past the Tompkins's farmhouse and the Wallace estate at full throttle. Annabelle tried to slow him down. But he was in no mood to follow the commands of his rider, whose voice grew louder as they neared the dead end of the gravel road. On either side, log ranch fences bordered muddy horse pastures. Ahead at the dead end, which Annabelle and Boomerang were rapidly approaching, a ditch and a barbed-wire fence fronted a thick briar patch.

I have no choice, Annabelle told herself. She jerked on

the reins, turning Boomerang hard left. *The fence isn't that high, so he should be able to clear it.* She was wrong again. His front legs made it over, but his back legs clipped the fence, causing him to stumble and fall. Annabelle rocketed off her saddle and somersaulted in the air. She tucked her body and pulled in her arms, as she was taught, and landed on the back of her shoulder with a splat in the gooey mud. Other than having the wind knocked out of her, she wasn't hurt and neither was the horse.

Boomerang scrambled to his feet and then stood still, his eyes wide. The saddle was heaving and his legs were shaking. He was wet with sweat, and the base of his ears was covered in foam.

Annabelle got up, wiped the mud off her clothes, and adjusted her helmet. She walked over to her horse, examined his legs, and looked for any injuries. She didn't find any. "Whew. We're both very lucky we're okay. But, Boomerang, really?"

That evening at dinner, the family talked about the horse's behavior. "We can't have him bolt like that," Norm said. "We're going to have to sack Boomerang out." He was referring to training the horse to handle common noises and disturbances so the gelding wouldn't panic over a sudden movement or unexpected loud sound.

The ranch had a holding stock similar to what veterinarians use for treating large animals. It was designed to keep a horse confined so it couldn't move around. Annabelle led Boomerang into the holding stock and then began introducing him to various objects and noises that might spook him. The first object, a white plastic grocery bag that was waved in front of him, caused him to whinny in fright. Annabelle talked softly to him and gave him several treats until he understood that the grocery bag wasn't scary at all. Before long, she was rubbing the bag on his face without him flinching.

For the next several days, Annabelle and her parents introduced Boomerang to different sounds: shaking a garbage bag full of aluminum cans, parading a neighbor's bleating goat in front of him, starting up a chainsaw, and letting neighborhood kids ride around on their bicycles. Annabelle even put her cat, Misty, on his back. With each new situation that Boomerang mastered, he received a carrot.

For the horse's final exam, her friend Jack Molina showed up in his ATV and drove it around the paddock. Boomerang was nervous at first, but soon relaxed and acted like he didn't care about the ATV at all. He had passed the test and was no longer a jittery, nervous horse. Over the next several months, Boomerang was a dream to ride, and the relationship between horse and girl grew stronger.

So when it came time for the Southcliff Equestrian Center's annual Halloween horse and rider contest, Annabelle naturally chose to ride Boomerang. To get that British punk rock look, she scoured several thrift shops and craft stores to buy studs, spiked belts, an awesome pair of leopard print pants, and a red Mohawk wig. She applied studs and spikes to a black jacket that she bought at a resale shop. Using black duct tape and peel-and-stick Velcro, she decorated Boomerang's bridle, reins, leg boots, bell boots, and leg bands with studs and spikes. She bought a Union Jack flag on the Internet for a saddle blanket.

Annabelle used ponytail holders on Boomerang's mane to give it a Mohawk style and colored it with red hairspray paint, which he tolerated just fine. She also painted his tail and attached inexpensive hair extensions with barrettes. Then, to hammer home the point, she used nontoxic washable white paint on his upper thighs and shoulders to draw several logos of punk bands, including a hooded skeleton, a glowing skull, and a symbol of a slam dancer. At her mother's suggestion, the girl took him for a few rides to test out the belts, boots, crazy mane, and tail. Boomerang seemed fine with the new punk look.

"It's a super costume," said her mother. "I doubt if anyone will top this."

"Oh, I'm sure Brooke will come up with something even better," Annabelle said. "She always does."

When Annabelle arrived with Boomerang at the Equestrian Center, the first person she sought out was Brooke. One look at Brooke and Nutmeg, and Annabelle knew she and Boomerang wouldn't win the costume contest. *Maybe if we're lucky, we'll finish second—again.*

Putting on a cheerful face, Annabelle said to Brooke, "You're zombies! That is just too cool!"

"Oh, thanks. I love your punk rocker costume. I think you're going to win this year."

"No way," said Annabelle. "It's not even a contest with your zombie look. I love it."

"Really? Thanks. I used special makeup for Nutmeg's rotting flesh. I dipped gauze in hot tea to look like dried blood and wrapped it around me. What do you think of my face paint?"

"You definitely are among the walking dead, Brooke. You're creepy. Very creepy. And so is Nutmeg."

As expected, Annabelle and Boomerang finished second in the costume contest—behind Brooke and Nutmeg.

However, Annabelle and Boomerang did collect one

first-place medal—when they teamed up with Brooke and Nutmeg in the pumpkin relay race. The first rider on each team held a pumpkin in one hand and trotted his or her horse from the start line to a barrel, circled the barrel, returned to the start line, and passed the pumpkin to a teammate who then did the same thing. Annabelle and Brooke were the fastest pair to complete the relay, beating out eight other teams.

When the horse show was over, Annabelle and Brooke rode their horses toward home. About a half mile from the center, they neared a trail that sliced through a meadow before it narrowed into the woods. As Boomerang started on the path, some boys in the field began flying a remote-controlled four-rotor video drone. Whether by accident or on purpose, the drone swooped low in front of the horse and then zoomed skyward.

Feeling Boomerang tense his muscles, Annabelle tried to calm him, but without success. He rocketed down the path and into the woods. *Uh-oh, he's lost it,* she thought. *Here we go again.* The girl tried everything to slow him down. She pumped on the reins. She seesawed the bit left and right. She leaned back in the saddle. She hollered at him to stop. Nothing worked, not even when Annabelle pulled hard on the reins, jerking Boomerang's head.

Because it had rained the day before, the trail was muddy and slick, but that didn't slow down Boomerang. Annabelle knew that at any moment, his feet could slip out from under him, causing a fall that could lead to serious injury or even death for one or both of them. *What more can I do?* she thought. Then she remembered a technique her father had taught her: turn the horse in a tight circle until you come to a stop. She was crazy to try it on such a narrow trail, but she had run out of options.

Annabelle reached low on the left rein and turned Boomerang's head, but he kept charging down the trail. She pulled harder. Soon she had Boomerang's nose pinned to her left boot so that his neck was shaped like a U. *This is insane! How can he still be running full steam with his nose aimed at his tail?*

Boomerang thundered on. *When is he going to fall and get it over with?* The anticipation of a terrible crash was weighing on her mind. And then it happened. He stumbled, lost traction in the mud, and pitched over on his right side. Like the smart young horsewoman she was, Annabelle let go of the reins, slipped out of the stirrups, and brought her arms close to her body. But before she had a chance to tuck into a ball, she slammed chest-first into the trunk of a tree . . . and then everything went black.

When Annabelle opened her eyes, she was lying in a hospital bed hooked up to an IV and monitoring equipment. Everything looked blurry, and her head and chest hurt. She couldn't move her left arm. Once her vision came into focus and she regained full consciousness, her worried parents hovered over her and offered her words of comfort.

They explained that the impact of striking the tree had broken her collarbone, knocked her unconscious, and given her a concussion. "The doctors say you'll make a full recovery," said Julie. "It could have been so much worse if you hadn't been wearing your helmet. Thank goodness Brooke found you and called 911. You were lucky it happened near the highway so the EMTs were able to reach you right away."

"What about Boomerang?" Annabelle asked. "Is he all right?"

Norm said, "Well, he's alive at the moment, but . . ."

"But, what, Daddy?" She didn't like the tone of his voice.

"When he fell, he slid in the mud and he got impaled on his right side by a tree branch that was sticking up from the ground. It collapsed his right lung and broke two ribs. It also introduced a lot of bacteria into his body."

"Oh, how terrible! Will he be all right?"

Norm hesitated. "Look, Annabelle, you know I'm a straight shooter, and I'm not one who sugarcoats things. You're a big girl now, so you might as well know the truth. Dr. Hamilton, our new vet, suggests we put Boomerang down because there's only a small chance for survival and he's—"

"No! No!" Annabelle protested, tears trickling down her face. "Boomerang has a strong will to live, and he's come so far after almost ending up in the glue factory. He's a good horse, a smart horse. It wasn't his fault he bolted. He was spooked by those jerks who were flying a drone. Please, Daddy, we have to save him. I love him."

Norm sighed and glanced at Julie. She nodded. "Okay, honey," Norm said to Annabelle. "We'll give it a try. But if the treatment isn't working or causes him more suffering, we'll have to put him down. And right now the odds aren't in his favor."

Her mother patted her and said, "The important thing—the only thing—you need to concentrate on is recovering. Now get some rest."

Boomerang was taken to the university's veterinary clinic for large animals where he underwent a delicate operation. He had to remain still and standing up while a surgical team spent an hour removing a thirty-inch-long, two-inch-thick branch from his body. The vets packed the gaping wound with four rolls of gauze and re-inflated his lung. They also inserted ports to drain fluid and they put him on several antibiotics to combat infection.

"The likelihood he'll survive is still slim," Dr. Hamilton told Norm. "But he tolerated the surgery quite well. We'll be monitoring him hourly. The first twenty-four hours are the most critical."

After spending a second night in the hospital, Annabelle, her left arm in a sling, was allowed to go home. She was groggy and nauseous from the concussion and in pain from the broken collarbone. Still, her one thought was about her beloved horse. "When can I see Boomerang?" she asked her parents.

"Once you're feeling better," said her mother. "In a few days."

Boomerang was not doing well. The medication wasn't killing off the infection like it should. The vets tried a different antibiotic, but the horse suffered a bad allergic reaction and went into respiratory distress and had difficulty breathing. "I think we need to prepare for the worst," Dr. Hamilton told Norm. "There's nothing more we can do."

When Norm told Annabelle about the grim prognosis, she sobbed. "I have to see him, Daddy! I just have to see him one more time before he . . ." She couldn't say the word *dies*.

Later that day, Norm drove her to the animal clinic. When she saw Boomerang, she was horrified and buried her head in her father's chest and burst into tears. The horse was standing forlornly in his stall with tubes sticking out of ports in his chest and sides. He was on an IV drip and on a feeding tube because he wasn't eating hay or any grains.

Dr. Hamilton took Norm aside and said, "We're doing all that we can, but it doesn't seem to be enough. I doubt he'll make it through the night."

Annabelle walked over to Boomerang. He backed away for a moment, as if he didn't recognize the girl with a bandage around her head, a black-and-blue swollen cheek, and one arm in a sling. But when he heard, "Boomerang, it's me, Annabelle," he nickered and bobbed his head.

With her free hand, she stroked his neck. In response, he rested his chin on her shoulder.

"Oh, Boomerang, I miss you so much," she said. "Please, you have to get better because I'd be lost without you. We have more trails to ride together. And we have to enter the Halloween contest next year because we can't let Brooke and Nutmeg win all the time. Come on, Boomerang, don't give up. I'll never give up on you. Get well, okay? And I will, too."

To the amazement of the vets, Boomerang survived the night. The next day, Annabelle returned to the animal clinic, spending an hour just talking sweetly to him about everything—the upcoming holiday season, her return to class, and her hope—no, *belief*—that she would one day be riding him again.

During her own recovery, she visited the horse about three times a week as Boomerang continued to improve daily. Soon the tubes were removed, the wound began healing, and the infection faded. As he got better, so, too, did Annabelle.

"It seems our medicine didn't work nearly as well as yours did," Dr. Hamilton told her.

"What do you mean?" Annabelle asked.

"Your love for your horse. I have no doubt your love helped get Boomerang through this difficult time."

Six weeks after the accident, when Annabelle was given the official word from her doctor that the collarbone had healed completely, Boomerang was allowed to come home. It took a few more months before the two could ride together, but Annabelle spent quality time with him, grooming him, singing to him, and feeding him treats.

When she began riding him, it was only in the paddock and for brief periods because they both had to regain their confidence. Eventually, they were riding, trotting, and galloping again.

Before long, the Halloween horse show was approaching. This time Annabelle was convinced she and Boomerang would capture first-place in the costume contest because she had conjured up a surefire winner—as the headless horseman on a skeleton steed.

Using cardboard and spray foam, she made elevated shoulder pads that sat even with her ears. Then, after donning an old extra-large black turtleneck sweater, she cut holes in the upper front for her eyes. She also made a cape out of black fabric. She planned to wear black pants, boots, and gloves, and, for a little extra flair, carry a scary-looking plastic pumpkin.

On the morning of the Halloween horse show, Annabelle and her mother used white nontoxic water-based craft paint and drew a detailed horse skeleton on Boomerang's sides, guided by a horse anatomy book borrowed from Dr. Hamilton. The painting took about three hours, but since the accident, Boomerang had been the essence of patience, so he didn't move or complain.

Shortly after Annabelle put on her headless horseman

costume, Boomerang acted surprised when he was told to stand still so a thing that sounded like Annabelle and smelled like Annabelle but looked nothing like Annabelle—or any human, for that matter—could climb aboard. Then the two of them trotted to the Equestrian Center, the confident rider waving to passing cars along the way. She believed that finally she would beat her best friend.

The contest was a slam dunk for the year's winner: Brooke Logan. Again. Brooke's dad had built a giant-sized rocking horse frame, which the girl painted in bright, bold colors. The frame had straps that rested on the back of her horse, whose body was covered with painted polka dots. With her hair in pigtails and wearing clothes and shoes that made her look like an overgrown toddler, Brooke licked a huge lollipop atop her "rocking horse" during the parade of contestants.

As usual, Annabelle came in second place. Sure, she was disappointed. But she didn't complain. After what she and Boomerang had gone through, she was content that they were even able to participate in the event together.

Besides, Boomerang would always be first in her heart.

The Ghost Cat of Edgewater Towers

The loud horrible sound sliced through the midnight hour like a high-pitched buzz saw before transforming into a long, grating shriek. Then, after a deep, eerie wail, it tailed off.

At first, Stanley Cohen thought this bizarre ruckus was part of a dream. But when he sat up in bed, he heard the unnerving sound again. "Mom?" shouted the ten-year-old boy, bolting out of his bedroom and into his mother's room. "What's that terrible noise?"

Having been awakened by the awful racket, Ava Cohen was already in her robe. "I have no idea, dear. It's rather alarming to say the least."

After a brief pause, the unearthly noise began again, increasing to an ear-shattering, hair-raising crescendo.

After Ava went from room to room, she opened the door of her apartment and peeked into the hallway. Nothing. "I can't tell where it's coming from," she said.

"Do you think it's a ghost?" the boy asked, his once sleepy brown eyes now wide open.

She rubbed his curly brown hair and flashed a reassuring smile. "Sweetie, you're getting caught up in Halloween. There are no such things as ghosts."

By this time, the strange sound was beginning to fade. Ava opened the door again and went into the hallway where mystified and concerned residents from three other apartments were huddled. She went over to talk to them. Stanley, in his red Roy Rogers flannel pajamas, followed her.

"It's what I imagine a she-devil sounds like," said neighbor Jerome Munson, a middle-aged man in a sleeveless T-shirt and striped pajama bottoms. "Or maybe a banshee."

"I think it's a baby with a bad tummy ache," added his wife, Dolores, her arms around two frightened preschoolers. "But I'm not aware of any babies in the building."

"It seems like it's coming from somewhere in the walls or ceiling," added elderly resident George Greenwald. "I'll be darned if I know what it is."

Mr. Munson looked at Ava and Stanley and said, "Quite a welcome for you two to Edgewater Towers."

"Yes, it is," replied Ava. She and Stanley had moved into the tasteful downtown apartment building eight days earlier, during the third week of October 1953.

"Um, is this sort of weird thing common here?" asked Stanley.

"Nope," said Mr. Munson. "Edgewater Towers is a great place to live, and we've never had any problems."

"Certainly nothing like this," added Mrs. Munson.

The door of apartment 3-A opened and out stepped a broad-shouldered man in his forties with slicked-back blond hair. He was wearing a dark blue silk robe embroidered with the initials *L.K.*

"Oh, boy, here comes Lawrence King," said Mr. Munson. "He's a big-shot banker and the head of our co-op board. A word of advice: You don't want to cross him."

"I've already met him," Ava said. "Thanks for the warning."

When Mr. King joined the group, he declared, "This has to be a practical joke—an ill-advised one. Teenage delinquents in this building would find it extremely funny to wake up and scare residents in the middle of the night. Halloween is only a week away."

Mr. Munson pointed to the Halloween decorations on the doors of the apartments on the floor and said to the Cohens, "As you can see, residents here make a big deal over Halloween."

"Much too big a deal if you ask me," Mr. King grumbled.

Mr. Munson continued. "A lot of families with kids live in Edgewater Towers, and as far as I'm concerned, they're all pretty good and well-behaved."

The disturbing noise didn't return, so the residents went back to their apartments. "Mom?" asked Stanley. "Would it be okay if I sleep with you tonight? You know, to keep you company in case you're still scared?"

Ava hugged her son and said, "I'd like that. But, please, no flopping around. I don't want to get bruises from your bony elbows and knees."

When the boy and his divorced mother had moved into the ten-story-tall, eighty-unit Edgewater Towers, Stanley had a good feeling about the place. He was impressed that the spacious lobby had been decorated for Halloween. Cotton cobwebs and giant plastic spiders covered the walls. Jack-o'-lanterns carved with grotesque faces occupied the corners of the marble floor. A fake human skull rested on the doorman's table, and a mannequin dressed like a green witch hung from the crystal chandelier.

Three days after moving in, Stanley had been waiting in the lobby for his mom. They had planned to meet his grandmother for dinner. Stanley, who was obsessed with westerns, was reading the latest Hopalong Cassidy ten-cent comic book, *Signature of Death*. He put it down when he saw a man in a blue business suit—who the boy would later learn was Mr. King—in an animated discussion with the daytime doorman, Mr. Brownstein.

"These decorations are ridiculous and don't belong here," Mr. King complained.

"But it's all done in the spirit of Halloween," said the doorman, a tall elderly fellow who always spoke politely even when he was miffed. "What's the harm?"

"This is supposed to be a fashionable apartment building, not some grade-school classroom decked out for a Halloween party. These decorations cheapen Edgewater Towers."

"They bring a smile to everyone who comes in here," Mr. Brownstein countered.

"Not to me or anyone with class," Mr. King growled. "I can't believe I was outvoted on the board to fund the money for this abomination." Shaking his head and mumbling to himself, he brushed past Ava, who had just exited the elevator.

"Mom?" Stanley asked. "What does *abomination* mean?"

"It means an eyesore or a disgrace. Why?"

"That man who just passed you was angry about the Halloween decorations."

"I was introduced to him yesterday. That's Mr. King. He heads the building's co-op board—the residents who make the rules—and he also lives on our floor in apartment 3-A." Looking around the lobby, she added, "I love the decorations."

When Stanley and his mother returned home after dinner, he noticed that of the eight apartments on the third floor where he lived, only his and Mr. King's unit didn't display any Halloween decorations. The Munsons' door across the hall at 3-G had a skeleton pinup, and the Greenwalds' apartment, 3-E, sported a poster of a funny-looking devil. The Cohens' next-door neighbors, William and Susan Hanover—an attractive childless couple in their thirties—had put up a sign that read MAY WITCHES BE KIND TO YOU ON HALLOWEEN. On a little table in the hallway next to their door sat a doll-sized skeleton clad in a black dress and a flowered hat.

Stanley went into his room and found a tablet of

construction paper in an unpacked box. He tore out a sheet of orange paper, cut it in the shape of a pumpkin, and drew what he thought was an ugly face on it. Then he taped the pumpkin to the front door. *There, now only Mr. King doesn't have a decoration.*

When the boy finished, his mother said, "Would you please return this pie plate to Mrs. Hanover?"

"Sure, Mom. She's nice, huh?"

"It was so thoughtful of her to make us a pumpkin pie and welcome us to Edgewater Towers. After you give her the plate, remember to say 'thank you.'"

When Stanley knocked on Apartment 3-C, Mrs. Hanover opened it, beamed, and said, "Oh, hello, Stanley. Please come in."

"Okay," he said. "Here's the pie plate. Thank you for the pie. It was really, really good."

"That makes me happy. By the way, you are coming to my party on Halloween night after trick-or-treating in the building, right?"

"Yes, Mrs. Hanover. I'll be going as a—" He was interrupted by meowing coming from another room. "Do you have a cat?"

Mrs. Hanover pulled in her shoulders and grinned sheepishly. She put her index finger to her lips and said, "I have a secret to tell you. But you have to crisscross your heart that you won't tell anyone except your mother."

"I promise," he said, crossing his heart.

"Follow me," she said. They walked into the kitchen, where Mr. Hanover was holding a string of red yarn that was being batted around by a full-grown cream-colored cat. It had blue almond-shaped eyes, a brownish triangular-shaped head, large ears, and a slender, muscular body. "It's a Siamese," she said almost in a whisper. "We call him Slinky. The way he moves reminds us of the toy."

"I thought we couldn't have pets in the building," said Stanley.

"We're not supposed to, according to the co-op rules," she admitted. "That's why you have to keep this a secret."

"How long have you had him?"

"About a week. My husband and I found him in an alley a block from here. He was shivering in the rain, all dirty, and didn't try to run away when we approached him. He looked like he was abandoned. So my gallant husband scooped him up, put him under his raincoat, and we sneaked him up to our apartment." She handed the boy a long piece of red yarn.

Stanley dropped to his knees and dangled the yarn. Slinky scampered over to him and began chasing after the yarn as the boy dragged it away. After playing on the floor for several minutes, Stanley said, "Slinky is a fun cat. He reminds me of Friskie—that was my grandma's cat. Before we moved here, we lived with Grandma for a while and I got to play with Friskie. About a month ago, he got sick and died. She really misses him, and I do, too."

"Well, feel free to come over here as often as you like, Stanley. Just remember, keep Slinky a secret, okay?"

The next two days after school, Stanley visited the Hanovers' apartment and played with Slinky. But when he went over the third day, Mrs. Hanover looked upset. "Slinky has disappeared," she told him. "I can't find him anywhere. When I last saw him, he was curled up in his little bed. I made him a place to sleep in the drawer of my dresser. I left to go shopping and ever since I came back an hour ago, there's been no sign of him. Cats are sneaky, but you'd think he'd come out, especially when I've been calling to him and offering him a treat. Will you help me find him?"

"Of course," said Stanley.

The two of them looked under every piece of furniture, behind the cushions of the couch and chairs, in all the kitchen cabinets, and even the refrigerator. They checked behind the curtains and the pillows and pulled back the bedding. No cat.

"The only thing I can think of is that Slinky slipped out of the apartment without me noticing when I left this morning," she said. "I can't imagine where he is." She was almost on the verge of crying.

"Have you asked other people in the building if they've seen him?" Stanley asked.

"No one else knows other than you, your mother, and my dear friend Mrs. Lyman in the floor below. Oh, and Mr. Brownstein. He's such a good man. He smuggled up a litter box for Slinky. We must keep this search a secret. If anyone finds out—especially Mr. King—my husband and I could be in a lot of trouble."

"I'll keep looking, Mrs. Hanover."

"Thank you, Stanley. We've grown attached to Slinky. He's such a loving cat."

In search of the lost feline, the boy scoured all ten flights of the stairway and then went outside and checked the alley without any luck. Giving up for the moment, he approached Mr. Brownstein and, making sure no one was within hearing range, told him, "Mrs. Hanover's cat got out of the apartment and is missing. I don't suppose you've seen a Siamese anywhere."

The doorman shook his head and said, "No, but I'll keep my eyes peeled."

It was two nights later when Stanley, his mother, and other residents on the second, third, and fourth floors were awakened by the frightening shrieks. The startling series of screeches and wails lasted only a few minutes that first night. But for short periods of time during the next day and the following night, the haunting sounds reverberated throughout the lower floors.

The building superintendent, Karl Werner, and several workers searched Edgewater Towers for the source of the nerve-rattling screams, but admitted they found nothing that could explain the sounds. Meanwhile, Stanley continued to sleep with his mother—you know, to keep her company.

Despite the unsettling mystery, the Halloween events at Edgewater Towers went on as planned. Stanley dressed as the Lone Ranger in a white cowboy hat, black mask, red kerchief, white shirt with a silver badge on his chest, a holster with a cap gun minus the caps, jeans, and sneakers. (He couldn't convince his mom to buy him cowboy boots.) He had used crayons to draw TRICK OR TREAT and DEAD OR ALIVE on the large brown paper grocery bag that he carried for all the goodies he intended to collect.

He knocked on every door in the building and gathered quite a haul. Then he went to the Hanovers' apartment, which was filled with adults and more than a dozen costumed children. Cowboys, hoboes, and ghouls played games with princesses, witches, and clowns. They bobbed for apples and took turns, while blindfolded, pinning the broom on the witch. Without using their hands, they tried to eat donuts tied to a string. And they played the popular Whirl-O Halloween Fortune and Stunt Game, which, depending on where the spinner stopped, required the contestant to do a trick such as balance a spoon on his or her little finger.

Stanley was ready to flick the spinner when a jarring howl that morphed into a shriek brought the festivities to a momentary standstill. After a brief shocked silence among the guests, some kids began to cry. Others began jabbering nervously and shuffling closer to their parents.

"They're like the screams of an old lady having a nightmare," said one mother.

"No, more like a werewolf," offered another resident.

"It's a prank," declared Mr. King, who felt obligated to make an appearance at the party even though he couldn't have cared less. "You don't see any teenagers here. Mark my words: They're behind this. And I intend to catch them."

"It's a ghost!" hollered Joseph Enders, the twenty-five-year-old part-time assistant to the superintendent.

Some laughed while others groaned at such a silly remark. Several guests, however, noted he was serious.

"No, really, it's a ghost—the ghost of a cat," Joseph announced, his face flushed, his eyes narrowed in torment.

"Why are you uttering such nonsense?" asked one of the residents.

"Because I should know," Joseph replied. He took a deep breath and said, "I'm the one who killed it. And now it has come back to haunt the building, to seek its revenge."

"What in the world are you talking about, Joseph?" asked Mr. Munson.

Joseph looked nervously at Mr. King and told him, "I have to confess, sir. I have to set the record straight. I'm at my wit's end."

Mr. King pursed his lips, nodded, and said, "Folks, Joseph might be right. This could indeed be a ghost cat."

"What?" said Mr. Munson. "Now look who's trying to pull our leg. If this is a joke, it's a bad one because you're scaring the little ones."

"I wish it were a joke," said Mr. King. "Let me explain. One night last week, I came down the stairs, and before

I entered the lobby, I saw the Hanovers talking to Brownstein. Then Mr. Hanover opened his coat and showed him a cat. They didn't notice me. I heard them say they found this stray and that they planned to keep it overnight. Even though this was against the rules, I figured one night wouldn't matter.

"Well, about three days later, I was walking by their apartment when I distinctly heard the cat meowing. This was clearly a violation of the building's rules—no pets—so as president of the co-op board, I took it upon myself to deal with this issue."

Turning to the Hanovers, Mr. King said, "I believed I was doing you two a favor, saving you from embarrassment of being exposed as violators. No doubt your conscience would have suffered terribly if you were to continue breaking the house rules indefinitely by keeping the cat. Because I have the power to investigate suspected infractions in this building, I had Joseph unlock your apartment when you were both gone and take away the illegal cat."

"You mean you had Joseph break into my home and kidnap my Slinky!" Mrs. Hanover shouted angrily, throwing her hands in the air in anguish.

Joseph, whose eyes were downcast, shifted his weight

from one foot to the other. He looked up at the Hanovers and said, "I'm so sorry. I was just following orders from Mr. King. I put the cat in a box and tied the box with string. I was going to take him across the river and release him on the other side. But as I was crossing the bridge, I wasn't paying attention and I got in the way of a messenger boy on his bicycle. He crashed into me, and the box flew out of my hands and went over the railing and into the water."

Mrs. Hanover unleashed a mournful cry, "How could you!"

"I swear I didn't mean to harm the cat. I didn't want it to die or anything. It was an accident. Two nights after the cat drowned, the haunting started. I told Mr. King, but he didn't believe the cat's ghost had returned. But when it happened again and again . . ."

"I am beginning to believe it," Mr. King admitted.

"So what are we going to do about it?" asked Mr. Munson.

"We could bring in a medium who might be able to get the ghost cat to leave," Mr. King suggested.

"We should fire Joseph," said a resident. "Then the ghost cat would have its revenge and leave us alone." His suggestion was seconded by several others.

"And Mr. King should move out, too," one of the guests shouted to cheers.

"I shall not," asserted Mr. King. "I carried out my duties as president of the board. I was enforcing the rules that we all had agreed to follow."

"I want you both out of my home right now!" demanded Mr. Hanover, who was spitting mad at Mr. King and Joseph. With his arm around his teary-eyed wife, he announced, "It's time for everyone to leave. This party is over."

As the guests were filing out, the upsetting caterwauling started up again. "It's the ghost cat!" a child shouted. Some of the youngest kids began to cry. Others screamed and ran for the stairway. And a few plugged their ears with their fingers.

Stanley moved into the hallway where the yowling seemed the loudest. As the boy passed a grated vent to the heating duct at the base of a wall, the screeching had reached a fever pitch. Even though he was scared, Stanley forced himself to kneel down and look through the iron grate. That awful noise stopped. And that's when he saw them—a pair of almond-shaped blue eyes staring directly at him.

"Aaah!" he blurted out, backing away. Then he looked

again through the grate and saw something moving, something cream-colored, something furry. It turned and faced him. There were those blue eyes again set in a brown triangular-shaped head. *It's the ghost cat!* thought Stanley.

But then it purred and rubbed its head against the grate. *Is it really a ghost?* After mustering up his courage—after all, the Lone Ranger wouldn't run off—Stanley slowly moved his trembling finger inside the grate. He was prepared for his finger to go right through the ghost cat. But that didn't happen. *I feel fur!* Then he felt the cat's sandpaper-rough tongue licking his finger, which was still sticky from the candy he had been eating. "Slinky! It's you!"

"Hey, everybody!" he yelled. "I found the cat! It's not a ghost! It's alive!"

The remaining guests crowded around the vent. But hearing the noisy kids spooked the cat, and he retreated farther into the duct. "I saw him!" Stanley exclaimed. "He's real! He's Slinky!"

Joseph kneeled down and unscrewed the grate that covered the vent. He reached in, felt around, and let out a yowl of his own. Joseph pulled out his hand, which was beginning to bleed. "That cat just clawed me!"

"You deserve it," Mr. Hanover said.

Suddenly, Slinky leaped out of the open vent, darted left, then right, weaved through the group, and sprinted down the hall with several people giving chase. At that exact moment, Mr. King opened the door of his apartment to see what all the commotion was about. The terrified cat, in his frantic effort to outrun his pursuers, scampered inside. Before Mr. King could do anything, Stanley and five other kids ran into the apartment.

"No, wait! Stop! Stop!" Mr. King shouted. But it was too late. Slinky leaped onto a side table, knocking over a ceramic vase, which crashed into pieces onto the hard-wood floor. Then Slinky bounded from the couch and onto the silk drapes. But his claws couldn't hold him up and he slid down, tearing the expensive fabric. Just as Stanley reached for him, the cat took off again. Stanley lunged for him, missed, and slammed into a planter. It overturned, spilling dirt and a miniature tree. Scrambling to his feet, Stanley snatched a small, decorative blanket off the couch and followed the kids into the kitchen, where they skidded on the tile floor, banging into a table and toppling over chairs. They finally cornered Slinky. In a last ditch effort to escape, the panic-stricken cat leaped onto the table and slid across right into Mr. King's arms.

The wild-eyed cat began clawing and scratching the man's arm and neck before Mr. King released him. Slinky flew off and onto the floor that was so slick the cat kept slipping, unable to gain traction. Like a fisherman with a net, Stanley tossed the blanket over Slinky and grabbed it. The cat howled and shrieked and pawed furiously at the blanket, but Stanley held him firmly.

"My apartment!" the bloodied Mr. King shouted. "Look at the mess in my apartment! Get out! All of you, out! Out!"

Stanley, followed by a parade of children and adults, returned to the Hanovers' apartment where Mrs. Hanover took the squirming cat and put him in the bathroom. "We'll keep him there until he calms down," she said.

"I think we all need time to calm down," said Mr. Hanover.

Slinky kept caterwauling. Although the racket was annoying, it was no longer scary, now that everyone knew it was coming from an upset cat and not a sinister ghost.

Few were more relieved than Joseph. "Thank goodness I didn't kill the cat," he muttered to himself. "Thank goodness Edgewater Towers isn't haunted."

The next day, Stanley visited the Hanovers to see how Slinky was doing.

"It took him two hours before he settled down," Mrs. Hanover told him.

"It's like he came back from the dead," Stanley said.

"We believe that when the cardboard box fell into the river, it broke open and Slinky got out and swam to shore," said Mrs. Hanover. "He obviously liked us because he made his way back to Edgewater Towers and somehow got into the basement and up into the area that houses the electrical wires and ventilation ducts. That's why we could all hear him when he started yowling."

"Are you going to keep him?"

"No, we can't," she said. "We and Slinky have created enough trouble. We need to find him a new home."

Stanley snapped his fingers and said, "I know the perfect place."

His grandmother was in for one happy, furry surprise.

The Lechuza

I know what I'm going to be for Halloween," said thirteen-year-old Elena Fuentes before taking a bite of her enchilada verde. "This will be the last time I go trick-or-treating because I'll be too old, so Jennifer, Mia, Lisa, and I decided to go all-out this year for our costumes."

"So, what are you going to be?" asked her father.

Elena took another bite, hoping to build suspense as the others around the family table—her parents; brothers Vicente, sixteen, and Felipe, fifteen; and their grandparents, who had come over for dinner—waited to hear her announcement.

"An owl," Elena replied. "But not some cutesy owl. A

scary one with a big head, glowing red eyes, a mean-looking face, big wings, and hairy claws."

"*¡Ay, Dios mio!*" her grandmother gasped, dropping her fork on her plate. "No, not that! Not a *lechuza*!"

"*Lechuza?*" Elena asked. "Abuelita, what are you talking about?"

"You've obviously never heard about the legend of the *lechuza*," said her grandfather Cesar. Referring to the Mexican town where he and his wife, Paulina, grew up, he said, "In Sabinas, people have always been afraid of *lechuzas*. A *lechuza* is a *bruja*—a witch—who can transform into a human-sized owl. She flies around at night terrorizing any poor soul she encounters."

"Are they real?" Elena asked.

Her grandparents responded at the exact same time, but with conflicting answers. Cesar said, "Of course not." Paulina said, "Absolutely, yes."

The boys snickered at their grandmother's response. "Really, Abuelita?" said Vicente, his eyebrows raised in disbelief. "Aren't you just saying that because Halloween is coming up and you're trying to spook Elena?"

Paulina shoved her plate aside, took a moment to look at each member of the family, and said, "I know *lechuzas* exist."

"Have you ever seen one?" Elena asked.

Paulina nodded. "I was tormented by one when I was your age."

Felipe burst out laughing. "Abuelita, you were attacked by Big Bird?" His comment triggered chuckles from everyone except Paulina.

"Laugh all you want, but it's the truth," she said. "*Lechuzas* come in all sizes. They aren't always as tall as a person. They often take the form of normal owls. But what they do to you is not normal."

"So what happened to you, Abuelita?" asked Felipe.

"One day in Sabinas, I was walking home from school on a narrow cobblestone street. There were no sidewalks. A mean dog came up to me and started growling and snarling and wouldn't leave me alone. So I picked up a rock and threw it at him as hard as I could. I missed. The rock bounced off the street and crashed through the window of a house. The woman who lived there was the owner of the dog. She saw what happened. And she was a *bruja*—that's what people said she was. I panicked and took off, and the dog chased after me. As I ran away, I heard the *bruja* shout, 'I will get you for this!'

"I was scared and confused and felt guilty. I didn't mean to break her window. I didn't say anything to my parents because I was afraid they would punish me. Instead, the *bruja* punished me."

"How, Abuelita?" asked Elena, who was so intrigued she had stopped eating. This conversation was getting more appealing than her mom's famous enchiladas.

"I was tossing and turning in bed when I heard a baby crying," Paulina continued. "That's one of the sounds a *lechuza* makes. I went to the window and saw the biggest owl I had ever seen in my life. It was sitting on the streetlight across from my house. The owl was staring right at me, and for the longest time, I couldn't look away—almost like I was in a trance. I knew then it was a *lechuza* and that the woman whose window I broke had turned herself into an owl. I closed my window, got back in bed, and threw the sheet over my head. Soon I heard a tapping noise. *Tap, tap, tap,* like someone was knocking on the window. I looked out from under my sheet, and it was the owl. It was hitting the window with its beak trying to get my attention. And it stared at me again. I swear, its eyes were red."

"Oh, Abuelita, please," said Elena's mother, Maria, who was Paulina's daughter.

"It's true," Paulina claimed. "For punishment, the owl continued to tap on the window and scratch at the windowsill, and cry like a baby. This went on and on. I hid under the covers again and was so frightened I didn't know what to do. So I started praying. And I kept praying for the *lechuza* to go away until finally all was quiet. I sat up in bed and saw that the owl was gone. Then I got brave and went to the window. I looked out and there, standing next to the streetlight, was the *bruja* and her dog. The *bruja* was staring at me. I ducked for just a second and when I looked again, she and her dog had vanished. It wasn't a dream, either. The next morning, I saw the windowsill. It was all scratched up. Never again did I walk down the *bruja's* street."

"Quite a story, Abuelita," said Vicente, shaking his head. He turned to Elena and said, "You're not buying any of this, are you? After all, this is the time of year for Halloween stories."

Elena shrugged her shoulders. "Abuelita wouldn't make this up." She asked her grandmother, "So what happened to the *bruja*?"

"Oh, she punished anyone who made her angry, whether they deserved it or not. She wasn't the only *bruja* who could turn into a *lechuza*. There were—and still are— plenty of them here in the Rio Grande Valley."

"Abuelita, we all know that's not true," said Maria.

"None of you believe me. Well, fine," Paulina said sarcastically. "Then how do you explain what happened a few months ago to Mrs. Estevez? She told me she and her two sisters were driving home from shopping at night on Highway 57 when they saw a huge owl in the headlights of their car. The bird flew ahead of them and was going faster than the car. Mrs. Estevez sped up because she wanted to get past the owl, but all it did was circle around the car and then fly alongside it right outside her window. She said the owl seemed to be mocking them.

"Then all of a sudden the engine stopped, the radio went dead, and the headlights turned off on their own. The car coasted to a stop. She couldn't get it to start, and they were stuck in the middle of nowhere. They were scared and locked themselves inside. The owl landed on the hood, and they could barely see it in the dark. It was staring at them. Then it flew off and Mrs. Estevez was able to start the car. That was a *lechuza.*"

"So *brujas* turn into *lechuzas* and harass anybody they want?" Vicente asked.

"No, only if they want revenge," Paulina replied.

"What did Mrs. Estevez do that made the *bruja* so mad?" Elena asked.

"She got into a bad argument with the owner of a dress shop, and Mrs. Estevez thinks that the owner is a *bruja* who turned into a *lechuza.*"

"Kids," said their father, "those are nothing but camp-fire stories. There is not a shred of evidence that *lechuzas* exist."

Paulina was miffed at the nonbelievers at the table. "There are many people who've felt the wrath of *lechuzas* and many who believe in their powers. I'm sorry if I scared you, Elena."

"Oh, you didn't scare me, Abuelita. In fact, you convinced me I made a great choice. I'm definitely going trick-or-treating as a *lechuza*."

Paulina threw her hands up in defeat. "Do what you want, Elena. I hope you won't scare believers—and I pray you won't anger a *bruja*. You don't want to make fun of a *lechuza*."

"That's enough, Abuelita," said Elena's mother.

Elena worked on her costume after school at the home of the most creative person she knew—her twenty-two-year-old cousin Yolanda, who was well aware of *lechuzas*. Although Yolanda thought the legend was silly, she personally knew people who kind of, sort of, believed in it. She had a big laugh when Elena recounted their grandmother's stories about the *lechuza*.

For the costume, the pair went online and studied photos of barn owls and drawings of *lechuzas* from websites about Mexican folklore. They fashioned a creepy over-sized owl head out of wire, papier-mâché, and oodles of feathers from old pillows. To give the face a spooky look, they created large, angry space alien eyes and a turned-down scowling mouth—both trimmed in red paint—and a black curved beak.

The wings were made from an old brown-and-white polka-dotted shower curtain cut in the shape of a cape with elastic hoops for Elena's wrists so she could unfurl her wings. From gray and white pieces of cotton fabric, the pair cut out patterns of feathers and hot-glued them to the back of the shower curtain. They also applied the cotton feathers to a ratty sweatshirt for the owl's chest.

They finished the costume a few days before Halloween. After Elena tried it on for the first time, Yolanda took several pictures on her cell phone. "You make a perfect *lechuza*," she said. Because it was dusk outside, Yolanda insisted on walking Elena home, which was only five blocks away. On the way, they took a lighted bike path that curved its way through a heavily wooded park.

Suddenly, an owl swooped down from its perch in the hollow of a tree and whizzed a few feet past Elena and Yolanda before landing on a limb about ten yards in front of them. "What are the odds of that?" asked Yolanda.

"We just finished making a head based on a barn owl, and now we see a real barn owl."

Elena stood still and studied the bird, admiring its beauty. It stared directly at her without blinking. Then Elena and her cousin walked past the owl and continued along the path, which bent into a sharp S-curve. They heard a branch move behind them and then, off to the left, the owl swept past them, only this time much closer—enough to make them both flinch. It turned and landed high in a tree behind them.

"It must be a *lechuza*," Elena joked.

Moments later, they heard a haunting, shrill hiss followed by a grating loud shriek that lasted about three seconds. They spun around. Gliding on long, slender wings, the owl zoomed low—too low—directly at Elena. She screamed, covered her head with her hands, and ducked. The owl's razor-sharp talons nicked both of Elena's pinky fingers, slicing open two small cuts.

"Oh!" Elena cried out. "That owl just attacked me!"

After getting a tissue out of her purse and handing it to Elena to blot the blood, Yolanda said, "It's trying to scare us."

In all seriousness, Elena asked, "Is it a *lechuza*?"

"Elena, don't even think such a crazy thought.

Obviously, the owl is protecting its nest. It probably has some babies."

The owl shrieked again, swooped down, and made another pass at them. They both screamed and dropped to the ground. "This is getting serious," Yolanda said. "I'm beginning to feel like we're its prey."

"Should we turn around?" Elena asked.

"No, we're almost out of the park. Let's keep walking, but faster."

As they warily moved forward, they kept their eyes glued to the owl. It glared at them as if daring them to go past. "Oh, no!" Elena cried out. "Here it comes again!" She went to her knees, whipped off her backpack, and held it above her head for protection. Yolanda did the same thing with her purse.

The owl's talons barely missed scraping them before it disappeared into a tree behind them. The pair began walking backward so they would have a few extra seconds of warning if it struck again.

"I'm really scared it's going to hurt us," Elena said.

"I don't think it will," said Yolanda. "If it wanted to hurt us, it would have dug its talons into us."

The owl did not harass them anymore. When they left the park, *lechuzas* were no longer in the back of Elena's mind. They were now front and center. *Maybe Abuelita was right, and I'm being punished for making fun of* lechuzas.

At the dinner table that night, Elena told her family about her frightening encounter with the owl. Her brothers laughed. "Abuelita warned you a *lechuza* would seek its revenge, Elena," said Vicente with a grin.

"All right, boys," said their father. "That's enough. Let's not say anything to your grandmother or we'll never hear the end of it, okay?"

That night, Elena was rethinking Halloween. *I don't have the money or time to make a different costume. Yolanda and I have put so much effort into making the head and wings, and they're so cool looking. But what if the owl is a* lechuza? *Will it attack me again? Oh, I'm thinking silly thoughts.*

Before going to sleep, Elena made sure the window in her room was closed and the shade was pulled down. When she woke up the next morning, she had made up her mind. She would go trick-or-treating as a *lechuza*.

On Halloween night, Elena donned her freaky owl head, shower-curtain wings, and feathery sweatshirt. She also put on hairy feet that she borrowed from her brother, who wore them as part of his werewolf costume in Halloweens past. She joined her three girlfriends—a one-eyed queen of the zombies, a gothic vampire bride, and a voodoo doll—and headed out to fill their bags with candy.

At almost every home, the adults who answered the door marveled at the girls' creative costumes. About halfway through the evening, the trio knocked at the home of an elderly woman. When she opened the door, she smiled at first, but when she saw Elena's costume, she stepped back and gasped. *"Lechuza?"* When Elena nodded, the woman uttered, *"Aaiiiyee,* no!" Then she slammed the door.

At a home on the next block, Elena received a similar reaction. The gray-haired man who answered the door told her, "Your costume is not funny. It brings up a bad memory." He pointed to a three-pronged scar on the back of his right hand. "A *lechuza* did that to me." He tossed candy bars into each of the girls' bags and closed the door.

Most people who saw Elena's costume assumed she was nothing more than a bizarre-looking owl and complimented her. But right before the girls called it a night, they stopped at another house. The middle-aged woman who opened the door took one look at Elena and said, "You're dressed as a *lechuza,* no? If I were you, I'd take off that costume and go home—if it's not too late."

"What is that supposed to mean?" Elena asked.

"It's dangerous to poke fun at *lechuzas*. For your own safety, do as I say and pray that a *bruja* didn't see you."

"Can we get our candy, first?" Mia, the gothic vampire bride, asked.

Rattled by the reactions of the three *lechuza* believers, Elena removed her owl head and strolled toward home with her girlfriends. As they neared the park, they bumped into the four coolest guys in their class, who were dressed up in *Lord of the Rings* garb: the Witch King, a Ringwraith, Gollum, and Azog.

After chatting for a little bit, the girls agreed to walk with them through the park. Elena wasn't too keen about it, considering the air assault the last time she was on the path, but she didn't want to be the spoilsport, so she stayed with the group. On the off chance that there were such things as *lechuzas*, she held on to her owl head rather than wear it.

About halfway into the park, they all heard a grating hiss followed by a screech. It was the barn owl again, and it swooped from its perch, aiming solely for Elena. Before anyone could react, the bird skimmed over Elena and tore out several strands of her hair with its talons. "Ouch!" she shouted, dropping her owl head and diving to the ground.

Seeing the owl pivot in the air and make another pass, Elena rolled up in a ball with her hands over her head, closed her eyes, and braced for another attack. Instead, she heard a thwack and then the boys cheering: "You got him!" "What a swing!" "Wow!"

Elena opened her eyes and saw the barn owl lying on its side on the path. Everyone had crowded around the bird. It was breathing but unconscious.

The Ringwraith, who was really classmate Julien Lopez, had swatted the bird out of the air with his plastic sword.

"Thanks, Julien," said Elena. "That owl really had it in for me. He attacked me and Yolanda yesterday."

"Yolanda told my mom, my sister, and me about it," said Julien, whose sister worked with Yolanda. "My mom believes in *lechuzas*, and she thinks the owl could be a *lechuza* because, you know, you're making fun of it with your costume." He took off his cape and wrapped it around the bird.

"What are you going to do with the owl?" Elena asked.

"I'm going to take it home and give it to my uncle tomorrow," said Julien. "If the owl survives through the night, my uncle will kill it—don't worry, he'll do it humanely—and then embalm it. He's a taxidermist. Then I'll be the only one in town with a stuffed *lechuza*."

"Thank goodness this *lechuza* isn't the size of a human, or I'd be dead," Elena said, shuddering at the thought.

"And all this time I thought my abuela was foolish for believing in *lechuzas*. At least this one won't be hurting me anymore." She shuddered again.

As they headed out of the park, Elena spotted a small hand-printed sign on a stake at the park entrance. It read: BEWARE OF AGGRESSIVE OWL PROTECTING HER NESTLINGS. TAKE PRECAUTIONS ON THE PATH.

Elena wondered, *Does that mean I'm not the only one who's been attacked?*

The group strolled with Julien to his house, which was only eight doors down from Elena's home. He put the still unconscious owl in a small pet carrier and left it in the garage.

That night in bed, Elena couldn't sleep. This whole *lechuza* thing was dominating her mind. She had gone from "it's nothing more than a legend" to "it's definitely real," especially after the second owl attack and the frightened reactions of the neighbors. But seeing that park sign cast doubt on her flip-flopped belief in the *lechuza*'s existence. *Maybe the owl isn't a* lechuza. *Maybe it's just nothing more than a mama looking out for her babies. If that's true—and I think it is—then she'll be killed for no reason at all, and her babies will die.* Elena jerked up in bed. "I can't let that happen," she said out loud.

Shortly after midnight, when everyone else in the house was asleep, Elena got dressed. She quietly picked up a flashlight from the utility drawer in the kitchen and tiptoed out the door. As she walked down the street, she thought, *I hope I'm not too late. I hope the owl is still alive.* When she reached Julien's driveway, she took a couple of deep breaths to calm her nerves. Then she sneaked into the unattached garage in the back, having paid attention earlier to where Julien had hidden the side-door key.

"Please be alive, please be alive," Elena murmured once she was inside. She aimed her flashlight at the kennel and saw the owl standing upright, its eyes open. "You're alive!" she whispered. "Oh, thank goodness."

Elena turned on the overhead light. For the first time, she noticed just how beautiful the barn owl was. She admired the way its flat, white face was framed in a rust-colored outline of a heart. She took note that its rounded head had no ear tufts. The bird's tan chest, which was speckled with black dots, reminded her of the poppy seed buns Abuelita often baked.

Seeing a pair of heavy-duty gloves on the work bench, Elena put them on and then slowly opened the cage door. "I'm not going to hurt you," she said in a soft tone. "I want to make sure you're not injured. Will you let me hold you, please?"

Carefully, she reached in. The owl kept staring at her, but didn't move. To Elena's surprise, it allowed her to pick it up and take it out of the cage. Considering the bird was the size of a small cat, Elena didn't expect it to weigh so little. The owl's hollow bones and powder-soft feathers made it look heavier than it really was. "Nothing appears to be broken," she said.

Gently stroking its back, Elena said, "I'll be nice to you and you be nice to me, okay?" She felt the owl tremble ever so slightly. "Don't be frightened," she said.

Sensing the owl was becoming fidgety, she set it down on the work bench. The bird immediately hopped onto her right wrist and turned its back on her. "Are you mad at me, or are you showing me that you trust me?" Elena said. Judging by the increasing pressure of the owl's grip on the girl's wrist, she said, "You're not as relaxed as you look, are you?"

The bird turned its head around and gazed directly into Elena's eyes. Its grip grew stronger. "I don't know what I'm supposed to do," Elena confessed. "Do I look away, or are we supposed to have a stare-down? Are you feeling threatened?" *What should I do? What should I do?*

And then a thought came to her. *This might be the stupidest idea ever, but here goes. . . .*

Elena closed her eyes.

She had no clue what the owl would do next. Its grip on her wrist remained strong. After Elena counted to five—she had planned to go to ten but couldn't stand being sightless any longer—she opened one eye and then the other. What she saw made her giggle.

The owl's eyes were closed.

Elena shut her eyes again. A sudden, unexplained feeling of peace enveloped the girl. She had no fear, no apprehension, no worries that the owl would hurt her. It was as though she had just plugged into an extraordinary connection between a human and a wild animal—a rare and wonderful moment shared by so few on Earth. *This is soooo awesome!*

She was willing to stay like this for as long as the owl wished—which turned out to be only a few seconds. Elena felt the pressure of its grip ease and its wings begin to move. "I know, I know. You want to get back to your babies."

With the owl still perched on her wrist, Elena walked in slow motion to the side door and opened it. As soon as the girl stepped outside, the bird flapped its wings twice, as if testing them, and then flew up onto a low-hanging branch. Illuminated by the light from the open garage side door, the owl fixed its gaze on her for just a moment and then cocked its head.

"I'll take that as a thank you," Elena said.

The owl then lifted off and vanished into the darkness.

The next morning, as students filtered into school, Julien rushed up to Elena, clutched her arm, and exclaimed, "Elena, the owl I knocked out was a real life *lechuza*!"

"How do you know that?"

"The owl was in a latched pet carrier in a locked garage when I went to bed," he said, his voice rising dramatically. "This morning, I went in there . . . and the owl was gone! The carrier was still latched, and the garage had been locked. There's no way the owl could have escaped without having special powers. That proves the owl was a *lechuza*!"

"Wow!" said Elena, faking surprise. She decided against saying anything else, thinking, *Why spoil the fun by telling the truth?*

The Witch's Cat

Lying on her stomach on her bed, Madison Welker stared at the screen of her laptop, trying to come up with a subject for her assignment to write a persuasive argument on a current issue. She was interrupted when she heard screeching tires and squealing brakes. She waited for the thudding sound of a collision, but it didn't happen. The only noise was a vehicle speeding off.

What was that all about? she wondered.

Madison rolled off the bed and looked out the window of her second-story room and saw a small black form in the middle of the street. *Oh, I hope it's not what I think it is.* She ran down the stairs and out the front door. When she reached the street, she winced. *Oh, it is.*

Sprawled on the pavement was a black cat, its legs straight out, its tail swishing in a jerky fashion. *It's still alive. What should I do?* She looked around. Nobody was outside. The residential street didn't get much traffic, although a different car was approaching. Madison put herself between the cat and the car, which was going the posted twenty-five mile-an-hour speed limit. She waved her arms and the car slowed down, made a wide berth around her, and kept on moving.

Seeing no other cars, Madison bent down and stared at the feline. Its eyes were closed, its tail had stopped shaking, and it wasn't breathing. *The poor thing. I can't leave it here.* She hustled back into the house, grabbed a towel, and returned to the cat.

She kneeled next to it and examined the vaccination tag on its collar. Engraved on it was SPOOKY, 1016 CHELSEA AVE. and the phone number. *Oh my gosh! It's The Witch's cat!*

At 1016 Chelsea Avenue, which was next door to Madison's house, lived The Witch. That's what the neighborhood kids called the reclusive, cranky woman. In an area where modest homes, bungalows, and Cape Cod-style residences were perched on small, well-kept lawns, The Witch's house stood out because it sat on the largest piece of property on the block—the equivalent of four lots. The house itself wasn't all that sinister-looking. It was a small, stone, one-and-a-half-story English cottage with a steeply pitched, gabled roof and a large chimney. It had tall, narrow windows and an arched, wooden door. The roof was stained from years of mildew and the brown, tan, and cream stones had a grimy, neglected look, much like the sprawling yard, which was pockmarked with bare patches and loaded with weeds and crabgrass. The bushes that bordered the house as well as the trees out front were in desperate need of trimming.

Over the years, Madison had spotted the black cat sitting on an inside windowsill between the always-drawn curtains and the window. It was never outside. Until now.

For that matter, The Witch was seldom seen outside. The rare times that Madison got a glimpse of her was when a middle-aged man in a nondescript white car would come over twice a week and pick up The Witch, presumably to take her on shopping errands. This same pudgy, balding man occasionally mowed the yard in the summer and shoveled the sidewalk in the winter.

For the kids on Chelsea Avenue, the evidence was overwhelming that The Witch was indeed a witch. From their perspective, she fit the profile: Her pasty face was slightly crooked and streaked by a scar from her right ear to the edge of her mouth. Judging by the way she kept her long, stringy, gray hair, it could have used a thousand strokes of brushing. She was tall and thin and always wore dark caftans and sandals—even in the winter.

The word was she was a single woman who never had children. "She didn't have kids because she hates them and puts curses on them, plus she's cursed and that's why she couldn't have any." At least, that's the explanation given by sixth grader Noah "Noah-It-All" Falkland down the street. "And she has to be single because no man is crazy enough to marry a real witch because she would put curses on him every time he made her mad."

And there was her name—Jennifer Salem. None of the kids knew what it was until the postal carrier accidentally slipped a letter addressed to her into the mail slot of the Welkers' front door a few years ago. (When Madison had been asked by her mother to deliver it next door, the girl admitted she was too scared, so her mom had to drop it off.) The Witch's last·name made perfect sense to the kids. Salem, Massachusetts, was where many of the famous witch trials were held in the late 1600s, resulting in the execution of twenty alleged witches.

The Witch was such a recluse that she had virtually no interaction with anyone in the neighborhood. And that was a good thing because, according to the kids, she would put a nasty spell on you if you angered her. On a triple dare, Noah had scribbled BEWARE OF WITCH in chalk on the front stoop and the next day—the very next day!—he broke his wrist while skateboarding.

Over the years, adults, like Madison's mom, tried to act neighborly by bringing over some homemade Christmas cookies or freshly cut flowers from the garden. On the rare occasions when The Witch actually answered the door, she would take the gifts, say "thank you," and close the door without further conversation. There were never any decorations during the holidays. And the house always remained dark at Halloween, not that any kid had the nerve to knock on her door and shout, "Trick or treat!"

That's not to say they ignored her on Halloween. Quite the opposite. Every year, the kids did something to her property: littered the yard with smashed pumpkins, TP'd the trees (some of which, by the way, were witch hazel), and soaped the front windows, to name a few.

But the clues that left no doubt at all that she was a witch were the skulls and bones. Kenny Turner and Skylar Vinson had seen them a year ago sitting on a table on The Witch's open back porch. The boys had sneaked into her backyard to retrieve a toy rocket they had launched. They counted about a dozen bones neatly laid out alongside two animal skulls. "They're probably from the dogs she ate," Kenny guessed.

When the woman stepped outside and saw the boys, she shouted, "Scat! Scat! Stay off my property!"

Yep, she was a witch all right. And for further proof? She lived with a black cat. Well, she *had* a black cat until it was run over.

Madison was kneeling on the pavement over The Witch's dead feline wondering what to do next. *I can't just leave it here. But if I take it to The Witch, will she be so upset that she'll put a curse on me? Remember what happened to Noah.* Despite her misgivings, Madison gingerly picked up the cat with the towel and cradled it in her arms like a doll. Its fur was soft and jet-black like Madison's shoulder-length hair. Repeatedly telling herself, *There're no such things as witches,* she walked up to the front door. *Just ring the doorbell, leave the cat, and run!* That's what she planned. But something inside her made her stay after she rang the doorbell. There was no answer. She rang it again. Still nothing. Then she started knocking loudly.

Finally, the door creaked open just a crack. "What do you want?" came a gravelly, annoyed voice.

"I, uh, am sorry to tell you, um, that your cat was hit by a car," Madison blurted out. "I'm pretty sure it's dead."

The door swung open, and The Witch stepped out onto the front stoop. She stared wide-eyed at the lifeless bundle in Madison's arms and shrieked, "Spooky? *Noooooo!* Not my Spooky!" While Madison continued to hold the cat, The Witch felt for a pulse, opened its eyes, and put her ear to the animal's chest. Her mouth open and contorted in anguish, she let out a silent scream followed seconds later by a rolling series of sorrowful sobs powered from deep within her gut.

Seeing The Witch start to sway and her knees shake, Madison quickly set Spooky down and grabbed hold of the woman before she collapsed. The girl led her into the living room and onto a couch where The Witch bent over, weeping and muttering, "Spooky . . . Oh, my dear, lovely, sweet Spooky!"

Madison scurried down the hall, found the kitchen, grabbed a napkin, poured a glass of water, and brought them both to her. "Please, drink this. You'll feel better. And here's a napkin for your tears."

Witches don't cry, do they? She must have loved that cat something fierce. Madison felt compelled to sit down beside the grieving woman. With some hesitation, the girl gently put her arm around her. "I'm sorry for your loss." Madison expected The Witch's heaving body to be ice cold, but it was warm just like hers.

"Oh, what I am I going to do without my Spooky?" the woman moaned.

When The Witch finished her crying jag, Madison explained that a hit-and-run driver had struck Spooky. "The body is by the front door," the girl told her. "Is there somewhere I should put it?"

"There's a freezer on the back porch. Could you put him in there, please? But first bring him to me."

Madison picked up the corpse and carried it into the living room. The Witch reached out, stroked the cat's head, and burst into tears again, saying, "It's all my fault. I opened the windows today just a little bit to get some fresh air. I must have opened one too much and that's how Spooky got out. Oh, Spooky, Spooky, Spooky."

Madison took the body to the back porch. When she opened the freezer, she gasped. Inside were the remains of various animals—a rabbit, snake, fox, and some others she couldn't identify. *Does she really eat them?* the girl wondered. She placed Spooky on an empty shelf and quickly closed the door.

It was then she noticed the bones of what looked like a large reptile on the back-porch table. As she stepped inside, she also spotted tiny bones and a microscope on the kitchen counter. Down the hallway, the walls were filled with framed drawings of the skeletons of various animals.

Madison entered the living room and asked, "Is there anything else I can do for you?"

The Witch wiped her runny nose and shook her head. Then she looked up and said, "You're the girl from next door, aren't you?"

"Yes, ma'am. I'm Madison Welker."

"Thank you for your kindness."

As Madison left, closing the door behind her, she thought, *The Witch doesn't act like a witch.*

Late the next afternoon, Madison saw the balding man in the white car pull into the driveway of The Witch's house. He opened the trunk and pulled out a shovel. *He's going to bury the cat,* she thought.

About twenty minutes later, curiosity got the better of Madison. She went over to the large hedge that separated the two properties and peered through the branches. She saw the man and The Witch standing over a freshly dug hole. Struggling to keep her composure, the woman looked in the hole and said, "Spooky, from the day I adopted you from the shelter, you were a wonderful companion—always there when I needed you. And I needed you a lot. Whenever I had a panic attack, you were by my side, helping to calm me. When I went into my bouts of depression, you would pull me out with your antics. I'm going to miss you so much." She began sobbing.

"Why don't you go back inside, and I'll cover him up," the man told her.

Madison felt sad for the woman and had an overpowering need to cheer her up. The girl went home, took a bouquet of flowers that her mother had brought home for the dining room table, and walked into The Witch's backyard.

The man had finished covering the grave when he spotted Madison. "What do you want?" he asked curtly.

"I'd like to give Spooky's owner some flowers."

"You mean 'The Witch,' don't you?" the man growled. "That's what you kids call her. You don't even know her name."

"Yes, I do. It's Miss Salem."

"Mrs. Salem," he corrected her.

"She's married?"

"She's been widowed a long time. I should know. I'm her son. Now, run along."

Madison stayed put. "I'm the one who found Spooky in the street, and I can only imagine how sad your mother is. I thought these flowers would cheer her up."

"She doesn't want to see anyone, especially a neighborhood kid. You've all been so mean to her."

"That's not true."

"Halloween last year? Her windows were soaped. Before that, the yard was covered with smashed pumpkins. Should I go on?"

She shook her head. "It's not what it seems. Kids are afraid of her because we've always been told she's a witch. She acts weird, yells at my friends if they step on her lawn, and she keeps bones. They're all animal bones, right? Not human?"

He snorted with contempt. "Yes, they're animal. Now, go."

"But these flowers—"

"I said leave."

As Madison walked away, she heard Mrs. Salem call out to her from the back porch, "Young lady, please come over here." When Madison did, the woman pointed to the flowers and said, "You brought those for me?"

"Yes, ma'am."

"Are you trying to butter up the neighborhood witch?" The smallest of smiles crept across her face.

"Yes, ma'am. I—I—I mean no, ma'am. I wanted you to have them. I wanted you to know I'm so sorry for your loss."

Mrs. Salem reached for the flowers and smelled them. "They're very pretty. Thank you. You're a nice young lady." And with that, the woman spun around, went inside, and closed the door.

That night at dinner, Madison told her parents why there were no flowers on the table.

"You did the right thing, honey," her mother said. "You've obviously made a connection with her when no one else has."

"I'm pretty sure she's not a witch," Madison declared.

Her father rolled his eyes and said, "Of course, she's not a witch. She's just reclusive."

"But the bones. Dad, they were everywhere."

"Okay, she's eccentric, too," he said.

Her mother said, "I have an idea. The poor woman is grieving, so I'll make her my famous tuna noodle casserole. You can take it over to her tomorrow after school."

"But, Mom, no. Let's just leave her alone."

"Nonsense. Everybody loves my casserole."

The next day, Madison rang Mrs. Salem's doorbell and then knocked twice before the door opened. The woman's eyes were red and swollen from crying.

"Hello, Mrs. Salem," said Madison. "My mom made this for you." She held out the casserole.

Mrs. Salem took it and said, "Why are you being so nice to me?"

"Well, that's what neighbors do for one another," Madison replied.

The woman hesitated as if she were wondering what she should say next. "Do you want to come inside?"

No, not really. It's scary in there. The bones. "Sure."

"Can I make you some hot chocolate as a thank you?"

"Sure, okay."

Minutes later, they were at the kitchen table. Bones were still on the counter along with a microscope. As uncomfortable as Madison was, she found herself oddly fascinated to be sitting across from this strange woman.

"You're the first person who has been in my house other than my son and the refrigerator repairman in the last year or so," Mrs. Salem said.

"But why?" Madison asked. "There are many nice people on this block."

Mrs. Salem sighed. "I have a condition. It's hard to explain, but it's best for me to go out in public as little as possible." She shook her head. "Let's change the subject. Tell me about yourself."

"Well, I'm in seventh grade; I'm captain of the soccer team; I'm on the debate team, and I love kayaking."

Pointing to the collection of bones on the kitchen counter, she added, "I guess you love bones."

"I was an osteologist—a person who studies bones—but I was forced to quit my job because of my condition. I haven't given up my love for the subject, though." She took a sip of hot chocolate and said, "Why I am telling you this?"

Madison shrugged. "Maybe because you want to."

"There's a kindness, an empathy, which radiates out of you. I can see it in your eyes. You remind me of my daughter, Rebecca."

"You have a daughter?"

"I *had*. Rebecca and my husband were killed in a car crash twenty-five years ago. My son, Henry, and I survived." Pointing to the scar on her face, she added, "This is a reminder every day how cruel life can be. Rebecca was about your age when she died." Her eyes began to water up. "This is when I need my Spooky—for times like this. I feel so lost right now without him. He was so much more than a cat. He was my emotional support when I would get these episodes related to my condition. He was always there for me. If only I hadn't left the window open . . ." Her voice cracked but she stifled any sobs. "I must get another cat—the right black cat—as soon as possible. I need one desperately."

Two days later, Madison was walking home from school on a sidewalk lined with birch, maple, and oak trees that were showing off their first hint of fall colors. She was lost in thought, still searching for the right subject matter for her persuasive-argument paper. When she was going past Mrs. Salem's house, the white car pulled into the driveway. Henry jumped out, hustled around the other side, and opened the door for his mother. She was weeping as he guided her to the front door. Suddenly, she dropped to her knees. Neither noticed that her purse had slipped off her shoulder, hit the ground, and spilled the contents. Henry helped her to her feet and brought her inside.

Madison dropped her backpack, ran over to the loose items, and stuffed them in the purse. Carrying the purse, she went to the front door, which was still ajar, and looked inside. She couldn't see anything but she could hear Mrs. Salem breathing heavily in the living room.

"Mother, you're on the verge of another panic attack," Henry told her. "You can get through this," he said. "Relax. It's unsettling but not dangerous. Now, breathe with me. One . . . take a breath . . . two . . . . exhale . . . three . . . take a breath . . . four . . . exhale . . . There, that's better."

Madison remained rooted on the front stoop, eavesdropping.

"Henry, how could the shelter be so foolish?" Mrs. Salem complained. "I went through the background check. They let me play with the cats, and the staff could see how instantly I fell in love with that black cat, Panther. And he bonded with me. We were meant for each other and yet they won't let me have him. It's senseless for me to wait weeks and weeks. Henry, I need Panther now. I don't think I can make it a month without him. I've had two panic attacks already since Spooky died."

Madison decided it was wrong to eavesdrop like this. She quietly was placing the purse in the hallway when Henry confronted her.

"What are you doing here?" he demanded.

"Mrs. Salem's purse fell in the yard, and I picked it up and brought it in. Is she all right?"

"She's fine. You need to leave."

From the living room, Mrs. Salem said, "Is that the girl next door?"

"Yes, Mother. I'm sending her off."

"Bring her in here, please."

Madison stepped into the living room and sat opposite Mrs. Salem, who was dabbing her eyes with a tissue. "It seems I've been thanking you a lot lately," the woman said.

"Are you okay, Mrs. Salem?"

"No, not really. I went down to Second Chance Animal Shelter to adopt a black cat and there was this one—his name is Panther—who won my heart. But they won't let me have him until next month. The shelter has banned all adoptions of black cats throughout October until early November. Today is October third. I can't wait four weeks."

"Why can't you adopt this month?" Madison asked.

"Halloween," Mrs. Salem responded. "They claim bad people adopt black cats around Halloween to use them as living decorations or props for their costumes or even worse, and then abandon them afterward. They also claim that black cats get sacrificed in cult rituals at this time of year."

"In this town?" said Madison. "I've never heard of such a thing."

"Apparently, shelters around the country are following this no-black-cat-adoption policy during October."

"Do you have to adopt a black cat?"

"Yes, I've always had a black cat since my condition developed following the accident. Spooky was my second one. I had him for fourteen years. Before him was Shadow. They both understood my problem and me, and they helped get me through the day. I wish there was a way the shelter would let me have Panther now."

"Mrs. Salem, I have an idea."

Madison went home and scoured the Internet for information about the abuse of black cats in the weeks leading up to Halloween. She learned Halloween originated more than two thousand years ago in what is now the United Kingdom, where pagans and druid priests started a festival known as Samhain. The festival was held every October 31, marking the end of the harvest season and the beginning of the coldest months. The priests said that deceased relatives would rise in the form of black cats during Samhain. Over time, superstitions led to the belief that evil spirits came out during the night of the festival, and the only way to stop them was to sacrifice animals. With their darting eyes and shiny coats the color of death, black cats became the sacrifice of choice because they were considered friends of the devil and mascots of witches. Ever since, over centuries, the black cat has been associated with Halloween and cult rituals.

"Although many shelter operators acknowledge having little or no first-hand experience with animal sacrifices on Halloween, they have long exchanged unproven tales of black cats being abused to mark the holiday," said one published report.

Madison looked further into the issue and came to the

conclusion that mistreatment of black cats during the Halloween season was much more fiction than fact. So, with her mother's help, she sent the following e-mail to the only shelter in town:

Dear Second Chance Animal Shelter,

You should change your policy that won't let people adopt black cats in October.

If you did your research, you would discover that black cats being harmed at Halloween is mostly a myth. Does it happen? Yes, just like it does other days of other weeks of other months. If you saw a tortured cat on December 10, would you ban adoptions because of the Christmas holiday? No, but if it happens anywhere in October, you blame it on Halloween.

I have spent a lot of time researching the number of animal-abuse cases in the course of a year. Do you know what I found? October does not have the highest number of cases. June is the most dangerous time. Many animals are injured, lost, or traumatized during July 4. Are you going to stop adoptions because of the Fourth of July?

October is blamed because there are more stories in the media about shelters banning adoptions of black cats. But there are few stories about actual abuses that took place in October compared to the other months.

I checked with your staff. Every person who wants to adopt one of your animals has to go through an extensive background check. They have to give their driver's license and ID, home address and phone number, vet information, personal references, and pay an adoption fee to get a cat. What difference does it make if that person wants to adopt in August or October? He or she still has to pass your test.

If someone wants an animal to abuse, why would they go to a shelter for one and give out all their personal information and pay an adoption fee? They know that you will be doing follow-up calls and checks in the weeks after they have adopted a pet. If these terrible people want an animal to torture, they'll trap a stray dog or cat.

Why am I asking you to change your policy? A very nice elderly lady, Mrs. Salem, came to your shelter two days ago and fell in love with a black cat named Panther. They had an instant bond. The cat needs a home, and this lady needs a cat to love. It's really, really important for her to get a companion right now. So why wait a whole month? That's wrong.

Your motto is "We are always on the side of the animals." Well, I urge you to show it by giving Panther a home right now with Mrs. Salem. Thank you.

—Madison Welker

The emailed letter worked wonders in so many ways. The shelter reversed its policy. Based on the positive background check of Mrs. Salem and staffers' observations of Panther's wonderful interaction with her, the shelter allowed her to take him home.

Meanwhile, Madison found the perfect subject on which to write her persuasive argument—against the banning of adoptions of black cats in October.

And there was a new development in the neighborhood: For the first time since anyone could remember, the front porch light was lit at Mrs. Salem's house on Halloween. Sitting on a table by the front door was a big bowl of candy with a hand-printed sign that said TO TRICK-OR-TREATERS: PLEASE HELP YOURSELF.

Some kids were still wary of going up to the house. But those who did collected their candy—and had a close-up view of a purring black cat sitting contentedly on the inside windowsill.

The Love
Bird

It was the strangest wedding any of the guests had ever attended.

For starters, the bride wore the tail of a fish. Actually, the shimmering, sequined aqua-colored tail was attached to the bottom of the bride's matching hip-hugging skirt. To cap off this Princess Ariel look, her long red hair was adorned with fake pearls embedded in seaweed and a headband made of stringed seashells.

Not to be outdone, the groom wore a tall, crooked green stovepipe hat that was decorated with a gold band of ribbon and sat atop an oversized bright-orange wig. His face was painted with silver makeup, and red eye shadow matched the color of his cheeks and lips. Clad in a shiny gold suit, this Mad Hatter wore a white satiny shirt and a huge blue paisley bowtie.

The maid of honor and best man were Raggedy Ann and Andy. Others in the wedding party included Pocahontas, Tinker Bell, Fred Flintstone, the pirate Jack Sparrow, and the Cat in the Hat. Little Red Riding Hood served as the officiant.

In attendance were zombies, garden gnomes, vampires, a giant pickle, Popeye, and assorted other inventive guests dressed appropriately for this Halloween wedding.

And—oh, yes—let's not forget the ring bearer, who was the one most responsible for Princess Ariel and the Mad Hatter getting hitched: a parrot named Ruffles.

Mark Hunter was walking to the park with his ten-year-old daughter Sophia, showing her around the neighborhood he had moved into following his recent divorce from the girl's mother.

"I've been here only a couple of weeks, but the neighbors I've met seem like my kind of people," said Mark, a strapping, tanned, thirty-two-year-old carpenter with a buzz cut. "They're always throwing block parties for any reason they can think of. Living here should be fun."

"I guess Mom was right about you," said Sophia.

"About what?"

"That you never want to grow up."

"That's not quite true, Sophia." He stopped, looked into the slender girl's blue eyes and said, "I admit that I play hard and like to have a good time. But—and this is important—I work hard, too." He rubbed her sun-kissed blond hair and said, "Remind your mother of that."

Ambling down the palm tree–shaded sidewalk along a row of small Spanish-style homes, he said, "Pretty nice area, huh?"

"Except for that one," said Sophia, pointing up ahead to a rundown two-story stucco house. Its walls were cracked, and the lime-green paint was peeling badly. The grass and bushes looked like they had been ignored for weeks.

As they strolled by the house, they were startled when they heard, "Help me! Help me!"

"It sounds like a woman in trouble," Mark said, looking for the source of the shouts.

"Help me! Help me!" the voice cried out. "No! No! No!"

"I think she's yelling from that yucky house, Daddy," Sophia said.

"You stay here," Mark said. "I'll check it out." He ran up to the weathered front door and could clearly hear the voice of a frantic woman. He tried opening the door, but it was locked. He banged on it and shouted, "Hello? Hello? Can anyone come to the door?"

"No! No! No!"

Mark hustled to the two partially opened louvered windows on the front and peered inside. He didn't see anything out of place—just some cheap-looking furniture and a messy coffee table. He ran around the back and tried to open that door. It also was locked. He pounded on the door but there was no response other than, "Help me! Help me!"

It sounded like the cries were coming from the slightly open window on the second floor on the front side. Mark whipped out his cell phone and called 911. "I'm at 525 Murray Road," he said. "A woman is in trouble inside a locked house. She keeps screaming for help. I can't get inside because the doors are locked and she's got louvered windows. . . . No, there doesn't appear to be a fire. Please hurry. She's really distressed."

Within three minutes, the first police cruiser arrived, followed moments later by a second cruiser, a fire truck, and an ambulance. The officers cautiously approached the house as the high-pitched woman's voice screamed, "Help me! No! No! No!"

After police announced themselves, they kicked open the front door and, with guns drawn, gained entry. The woman's cries suddenly stopped as officers cautiously checked the entire house, room-by-room on both floors trying to locate the source of the screams and a possible suspect. They couldn't find any victim or culprit.

A police sergeant walked over to Mark, who was standing with Sophia on a sidewalk where neighbors had gathered, and asked him, "Are you the person who called 911?"

"Yes, sir."

"Well, we can't find anyone inside, and we searched the premises pretty thoroughly. There's no one. The only living thing in the house is a bird in a cage."

"Is it a parrot?" Mark asked.

The officer shrugged. "I guess. It's a decent-sized gray bird with a black beak. Why?"

"You're describing an African grey parrot," Mark said. "A bird like that can imitate people and sounds. My family had a parrot when I was a kid. Mind if I check it out?"

The officer led Mark into the house and up the stairs to a bedroom where a caged parrot ruffled its feathers, hopped around, and then shrieked, "Help me! Help me!"

As other police officers scrambled into the room, Mark chortled, "Well, there's your culprit—and your victim."

"I can't believe it," said the sergeant. "That bird sounds just like a screaming woman."

Mark walked out of the house and rejoined Sophia. He was explaining to her and the small group of neighbors about the feathered drama queen when a muscular, tattooed bald man pulled up on his motorcycle.

"That's Rick Lauer," said a neighbor. "He's bad news."

Upset that the police had broken into his house, Lauer erupted in a foul-mouthed tirade against the sergeant. One word led to another, and suddenly the police slapped handcuffs on Lauer. When they did an on-the-scene background check, they discovered several warrants were out for his arrest on felony charges. As they led Lauer to a squad car, Mark shouted, "What about the parrot? You can't leave it alone."

Lauer hollered back, "He's more trouble than he's worth. I don't want him anymore. Take him. He's yours."

And so Mark wound up with a winged roommate—a ten-year-old male African grey parrot named Ruffles.

Had the neighbors on either side of Lauer's house been home at the time, they would have told Mark not to bother calling the cops. They would have explained that Lauer had inherited the bird several weeks earlier from his deceased mother. She had lived alone in another town and had taught Ruffles to scream like a human in case the bird ever felt threatened or sensed his owner was in danger.

That's all Mark learned about the bird. Fortunately, Mark knew all about the proper care and feeding of a parrot, having grown up in a household that had one named Spike. Spike was affectionate toward all the members of the family, but favored Mark's sister, Nancy, who ultimately took the bird with her after she got married.

Ruffles adapted quickly to his new surroundings in Mark's two-bedroom house. It took Mark a little longer to adapt to Ruffles's many quirks and talents. For one thing, the parrot could swear like an angry drill sergeant—a habit he no doubt picked up from Lauer. The bird also had an amazing ability to imitate other animals. He could quack like a duck, gobble like a turkey, and hoot like an owl. He could also snort like a pig, bark like a dog, and meow like a cat.

Often, Ruffles would wake up at sunrise and crow like a rooster. Other times, the bird crowed just because it was a fun noise to make. Once when Sophia was spending the weekend with her dad, she forgot to latch the bird's cage at night. When Ruffles woke up early the next morning, he got out of the cage, waddled over to the girl's partially closed bedroom door, and pushed it open. Then he climbed the bed covers, hopped right up to the girl's face and let loose with an ear-splitting cock-a-doodle-doo that jolted Sophia so much she tumbled off the bed. Despite that rude awakening, Sophia loved spending time with the parrot, and the feeling was mutual.

Mark began putting Ruffles on his shoulder and taking him to parties, get-togethers, and for walks in the park with Sophia. "Ruffles enjoys attention," Mark told her. "I feel that exposing him to the outside world is making him a sweeter and more sociable bird."

Ruffles had become the neighborhood celebrity—and a chick magnet for Mark. The bird had a knack for attracting women who would come up to Mark and start a conversation. Usually it would go something like this:

Woman: Oh, what an adorable parrot. Does your bird talk?

Mark to Ruffles: What do you say to this young lady, Ruffles?

Ruffles: Hello. How are you? You're pretty.

The encounter sometimes led to a date. Ah, but Mark also got burned occasionally by those embarrassing moments when Ruffles was in one of his naughty moods. Upon meeting someone, the parrot would either laugh hysterically or, for some unknown reason, shout, "Baloney!" And then there were those really uncomfortable times— fortunately, not too often—when Ruffles would show off his vocabulary of bad words.

Mark was never quite sure what the parrot would do whenever he brought a date home. Usually, Ruffles behaved himself—but not always. He developed a habit of saying in a low voice, "Oh, baby, baby." If Mark and his date were sitting on the couch, Ruffles was just as likely to imitate a gross belch or burp as he was to make a smacking, kissing sound.

When it was time for the Murray Road Halloween block party, Mark dressed up as a couch potato. He built a lightweight frame shaped like a sofa and covered it in a tacky plaid fabric. He cut a hole in the seat, allowing him to slip the sofa over his head. He attached shoulder straps so he could wear the whole thing around his waist like a life preserver. Then he glued a potato chip package, a soft drink bottle, a can of peanuts, a TV remote, candy-bar wrappers, and a chip-dip container onto the "couch."

Sophia went as a movie-theater floor. She wore a black cap, a black, long-sleeve T-shirt, and black tights, and glued crushed plastic cups, candy wrappers, a smashed popcorn box, crumpled napkins, bent straws, and gobs of chewed gum on them. Stuck to her chocolate-smudged face were about a dozen popcorn kernels.

And as for Ruffles? He sat on Mark's shoulder wearing a little picture around his neck of an alarm clock showing the time as 5 A.M. Yep, he was going as the early bird. Mark hoped Ruffles would be willing to keep a fake worm in his mouth. You know, the early bird catches the worm. But the parrot refused.

The couch potato and the movie-theater floor joined hundreds of other Halloween celebrants along a closed-off five-block stretch of Murray Road. Other than the residences of a few spoilsports and the now-empty house of that bad guy, Lauer, almost every home featured ghoulish and clever Halloween decorations. To collect her treats, Sophia navigated through a few graveyard front lawns, walked under ghosts and goblins dangling from trees, skipped past spooky jack-o'-lanterns and skeletons, and marched up to houses that had bizarre faces peering out from windows. The most creatively decorated house featured a large crashed UFO with a dead alien sprawled on the front yard.

While keeping tabs on Sophia, Mark was celebrating

with costumed neighbors like Mad Max, the Cheshire Cat, a Rubik's Cube, Beyoncé (a woman in a bee costume with sparkly letters that spelled out "Yoncé"), Optimus Prime, and a lightning strike (a guy dressed as a lightning bolt and his frizzy-haired girlfriend wearing torn, burned clothes).

Ruffles reveled in all the attention and excitement during the first hour but eventually the growing crowd and the screaming kids began making him edgy and uncomfortable. So when one of Mark's buddies, who was a scary zombie clown, suddenly leaped in front of Mark, Ruffles let out a frightened shriek and flew off into the darkness.

After asking a friend to look after Sophia, Mark threw off his couch-potato costume and started sprinting after the parrot. Mark had lost sight of his pet, but kept running in the general direction that he last spotted him. Meanwhile, several friends spread out and searched for the bird, too.

No one could find Ruffles. About four blocks away on quiet Webster Avenue, Mark spotted a petite woman in her thirties, staring up at a banyan tree. She was obviously in the Halloween spirit because she was dressed as a businessman caught in a hurricane.

She was carrying a tattered umbrella that was turned inside out. Her red hair had been hair-sprayed back for a windblown effect. Her necktie had a wire through it so that the tie was suspended over her shoulder, giving the illusion that it had been caught by a gust. To further add to the impression that she was getting blasted by the wind, she had glued a page from a newspaper, leaves, and litter to her pants and open sport coat.

Mark ran up to her and said, "Have you seen or heard a parrot?"

Pointing to the banyan tree, she replied, "Yes. I saw a parrot fly in there a few minutes ago. I stopped and tried talking to it, and it shouted back, 'No! No! No!' And then," she added with a giggle, "it said a string of swear words."

"That's got to be Ruffles, my pet African grey. He freaked out at the block party and flew away." Craning his neck, Mark couldn't see anything beyond the first few branches because it was too dark. He called out anyway in a reassuring voice. "Ruffles, Ruffles. It's me, Mark. Everything is going to be all right. Come down here. Come to me." In the dim light from the nearby street lamp, Mark spotted movement on a low-hanging branch. "I see you! I see you!" Turning to the woman, he said, "Well, that's half the battle. At least I know where he is."

The parrot screamed and then uttered a few more swear words.

"Your pet has quite the vocabulary," the woman said.

"He didn't learn it from me."

Just then, a plop of bird poop landed on the woman's shoulder. She laughed and said, "And he has quite an aim, too."

"I'm so sorry. Ruffles is obviously upset. It was a mistake to bring him to the Halloween block party."

"That's where I was going," she said, moving out into the street and away from the branch where Ruffles perched.

"Oh, please, I don't mean to hold you up. It's quite a party—or it was for me until this happened."

"How are you going to get him down?"

"I have to show patience," Mark replied. "He sees me. He'll come down when he's good and ready. It just might take a while."

Now that the woman was away from the shadows, her face was illuminated by the streetlight. For the first time, Mark had a good look at her—short, fit looking, and blessed with a freckled pixie face. Even with her sprayed hair and smudged face, he thought, *Wow, she's pretty. And she has a great smile and giggle.* He held out his hand and said, "My name is Mark Hunter."

"Hello, Mark Hunter. I'm Shannon Mahoney. Nice to

meet you." Flicking off the remainder of the bird poop on her shoulder, she added, "And I've already met Ruffles."

Over the next ten minutes, the two of them sat on the ground under the banyan—but out of Ruffles' bombing range—and chatted. During that brief time, Mark learned that Shannon had moved into a nearby apartment with her two Siamese cats, Tweedle Dee and Tweedle Dum, the previous month. Divorced with no kids after a brief marriage, she worked as a medical lab technician. For fun, she scuba dived, fished, and played midfielder on a winning team in a women's soccer league.

An obvious mutual attraction was blooming between the two—a development that wasn't lost on Ruffles. From his perch on the branch, he started making kissing sounds before transitioning into a low-voiced "Oh, baby, baby." Shannon and Mark burst out laughing, partly to cover up their embarrassment.

"Ruffles, come on down," Mark coaxed. "It's time."

The parrot agreed. Ruffles left the branch and glided onto Mark's shoulder. "Good bird," said Mark, gently stroking the bird's head. "I want you to meet my new friend. Her name is Shannon. Ruffles, can you say hello?"

"Oh, baby, baby," the bird said, causing the two to crack up again.

After Shannon stopped chuckling, she pet the parrot, who began making kissing sounds again.

"I think he wants to give you a kiss," Mark told Shannon.

Somewhat unsure, she moved closer to the bird and puckered her lips. At that exact moment, one of Mark's friends who had been searching for Ruffles, turned the corner, saw Mark, and hollered out to him. Spooked by the shout, Ruffles flapped his wings and clamped his beak right on Shannon's nose. Naturally, she screamed in pain. Mark twisted around, grabbed the bird, and made Ruffles let go.

"How could you?" Mark scolded the parrot. "No, Ruffles! No!"

"No! No! No!" the bird shrieked. "Help me! Help me!" Then the parrot unleashed another barrage of swear words.

Geez, can things get any worse? Mark thought. "Shannon, are you hurt?"

Holding her nose with both hands, she shook her head and said, "I'll be okay, although I might not be stopping to smell the roses anytime soon."

"I am so sorry. Ruffles just isn't himself right now. I apologize. Please, Shannon, you've got to give me a chance to make this up to you."

It was, by far, the craziest way Mark ever made a date—one that turned into a second date and then a third and so on until he and Shannon fell in love. To their circle of friends, they were the wacky couple who loved to throw theme parties: come-as-you-are; rockin' fifties; Kentucky Derby; Mardi Gras; St. Patrick's Day. The pair were like-minded kids at heart. Sometimes, when they went out to eat, they would talk in fake accents or carry on nonsensical conversations that were meant for other patrons to hear and become totally perplexed.

Fortunately, Shannon's outgoing personality and humor matched Sophia's. As Mark's relationship with Shannon deepened, Sophia's bond with Shannon grew stronger. And despite the rather awkward and mortifying first impression that Ruffles had made on Shannon, she and the bird became good friends. But he still embarrassed her from time to time.

On occasion, when she introduced a friend of hers to him, Ruffles would belch or burp, and the first time he greeted her parents, he shouted, "Baloney!" Then, there was that memorable day at the soccer game.

Mark had taken Ruffles to several of Shannon's matches, having taught the bird to shout, "Go, Shannon, go!" But during this one particular game, the parrot began imitating the referee's whistle. The first time the players heard it, they stopped playing because they assumed there had been a penalty or injury. But the referee signaled for the players to carry on. The same thing happened again. After the third time, the referee went into the bleachers where the parrot was sitting on Mark's shoulder. The ref told the spectators, "Whoever is blowing the whistle, stop it right now!"

"Hey, ref, it's not any of us," Mark said. "It's my parrot."

"Go, Shannon, go!" Ruffles said, before imitating the whistle again.

Everyone—the ref, the players, the spectators—roared with laughter. Still snickering, Shannon went over to the bird and said, "Ruffles, you goofy parrot. No more whistles."

The ref told Mark, "This is one for the books, but you need to take that bird out of here or else I'll forfeit the game to the other team."

Shannon placed her hands on each side of her reddening face. Referring to the penalty card for ejection in a soccer match, she moaned to her teammates, "I don't believe this. My boyfriend's parrot just got red-carded!"

About eight months after Mark first met Shannon, he decided to propose to her. He had already received approval from Sophia, who had earlier come to terms that her parents were never getting back together even though they had remained friends after the split-up.

Mark wanted the proposal to be different and unusual—and involve Ruffles. So he trained the parrot for a special night.

Shannon arrived at Mark's house for a candlelit dinner. He prepared the entire meal and, in fact, had caught the main dish—red snapper, which was one of her favorite fish to eat. After a dessert of crepes suzette (which he had made for the first time), he called Ruffles over to the table. On Mark's command, the bird used his beak to push a small wooden box across the table to Shannon.

"What in the world is this?" Shannon asked.

"Ruffles has something to say on my behalf," Mark said.

A small ribbon was attached to the lid of the box. The parrot used his beak to yank the ribbon and open the lid, revealing a diamond engagement ring. "Will you marry me?" Ruffles said. "Marry me?"

Shannon sat motionless in her chair, showing no expression although tears were welling up in her eyes. Then she flashed a huge smile and blurted, "Yes!" Shannon reached for the diamond ring and then stopped. "Wait," she said with her head cocked. "Just to be clear,

Mark. I'm saying yes to marrying you, and not Ruffles, right?"

"It's your call," he replied with a wink. "Ruffles has some fine qualities, but overall, I think I'm the better catch."

As the two stood up to embrace, Ruffles began making those goofy kissing sounds.

There was absolutely no disagreement, no second thoughts about when to get married. They both knew there was only one perfect date for their wedding— October 31, exactly a year from the night they first met, thanks to Ruffles. In keeping with their penchant for theme parties, they decided they would have a Halloween wedding and reception. Everyone, including the bride and groom, had to come in costume.

And so on Halloween night, Princess Ariel and the Mad Hatter stood in the VFW Club's event room in front of the celebrant, Little Red Riding Hood. Standing behind Raggedy Ann and Andy, Sophia was dressed as a female Jack Sparrow. She was in charge of Ruffles, who had an important role to play in the ceremony. He perched on her shoulder.

"We have come together on this festive holiday to bless the marriage of Shannon Erin Mahoney and Mark

Edward Hunter," said Little Red Riding Hood. "Shannon and Mark, your family and friends are here to celebrate your love on this wonderful holiday. In the ancient days of the Celts, Halloween was believed to be a brief moment when all laws of time and space were suspended for the evening, and the spirit world and our world were one. According to legend, the veil between the two worlds is at its thinnest on Halloween night. It is a time when spirits intermingle with the living. The tradition of wearing costumes is to confuse those spirits who may want to do us harm. Yet for us, here and now, this night is all about love and merriment and treats—and maybe some trickery."

After the celebrant finished with her address and the couple said their vows, it was time for the exchange of wedding rings. With a ring attached to each of his legs, Ruffles flew from Sophia's shoulder to Mark's arm. Then Shannon removed the rings from the parrot's legs.

Slipping a ring onto Shannon's finger, Mark recited, "As this ring encircles your finger from this day forward, year in and year out, so will my love forever encircle you."

Just then, as if on cue, Ruffles said in low voice, "Oh, baby, baby."

The Cemetery Dog

For sixteen-year-old Connie Graham, the Halloween of 1948 was a time for revenge after what happened to her the year before.

In her circle of friends at Rock Island High School, none was as trusting or easily fooled as Connie. The soft, baby-faced brunette was an easy target for fun-loving pranksters because she was so gullible. Egged on by Rudy Lund, who was her new boyfriend, Connie was willing to consider some form of retaliation against those responsible for the previous year's borderline-nasty Halloween prank that had given her nightmares for weeks.

Back then, against her better judgment, Connie had gone with a small group of friends to the funeral home owned by the father of classmate John Bengston. Without the owner's consent, the kids sneaked into the home, supposedly to conduct a séance with John as the medium. He had claimed he could get in touch with the recently deceased grandmother of Connie's friend Joyce Peterson. The group sat around a table in the darkened casket showroom, which was illuminated by a sole candle. John went through the motions and incantations to make contact with the "grandmother," whose eerie voice was really Sally Wentford, who was hiding behind a coffin and whispering through a megaphone. Everyone but Connie was in on the joke. Although Connie was scared, she was also intrigued because Joyce was communicating with "Grandma."

But then "Grandma" became agitated and claimed an evil force had just taken over the soul of a deceased man whose body lay in one of the caskets in the room. Suddenly, the lid of the casket sprung open, and a man (really John's older brother, Brian) in ghastly makeup sat upright. Connie screamed in terror, wet her pants, and bolted out of the funeral home. For days afterward, she had to put up with a constant stream of ribbing and puns, all said with straight faces: "Hope you weren't too pee-trified." "That was an awful prank played against you, and I'm dead serious." "I have a tinkling of a notion that you were a wee-wee bit upset."

Now, at Rudy's urging, Connie was plotting to get even during the upcoming Halloween. She found out the previous year's pranksters were going to pull a similar trick on classmate Debbie Krueger, only this time at the Chippiannock Cemetery (pronounced *chip-EYE-an-nock*). With the help of six college students from Augustana College, Connie planned to scare the pants off the pranksters (figuratively speaking)—and have them photographed while fleeing in terror. To finalize her scheme, she and Rudy went to the cemetery in the afternoon a week before the big night.

The sprawling cemetery of thousands of gravestones, located on a rolling hillside in Rock Island, Illinois, was nearly one hundred years old. Its name meant "village of the dead" in the Native American language of the Sauk and Fox tribes who lived on the land hundreds of years earlier. The cemetery was the final resting place for local Civil War generals, congressmen, and businessmen, as well as murderers, bootleggers, and everyday folks.

When Connie and Rudy arrived at the cemetery after school, they began scouting for the perfect spot to carry out their prank. Shortly after passing a large monument featuring the statue of a mourning woman, they noticed a stout, gray-haired lady ahead of them. She was dressed in an expensive powder-blue wool overcoat and a matching flowery silk head scarf. Both hands were adorned with diamond rings. While clutching a black leather purse in her left hand, she was leaning with her right on an elaborately carved cane when she stumbled and fell in the grass. The two rushed over to help her.

"Are you hurt?" Connie asked as Rudy helped the woman to her feet and fetched her glasses and scarf.

"I—I'm not sure," she answered with a dazed look. "Is this where I catch the bus?"

"Oh, dear, you seem confused," Connie said. "You're in the Chippiannock Cemetery."

"Well, I don't think I'm ready for this place just yet," said the woman, somewhat indignantly.

"Should I get some help for you?" Rudy asked.

"If you could assist me to that bench over there, I would be most grateful."

Rudy and Connie each took an arm and guided her over to the bench. "Thank you kindly," said the woman. To Rudy, she said, "You look familiar. Are you a policeman?"

"No, ma'am. I'm in high school. Say, aren't you Mrs. Abbott?" When she nodded, he said, "I'm Rudy Lund, a friend of Walter Abbott, your great-grandson. I've met you a few times at Walter's house."

"Oh, really? If you say so." Mrs. Abbott closed her eyes for a moment and took a deep breath. Rudy gazed at Connie with a concerned expression. By the way Mrs. Abbott was impeccably dressed, it was obvious she was a refined woman of wealth even if she was apparently senile.

When the woman opened her eyes, she smiled and no longer appeared nearly as bewildered as she had moments earlier. "It's no fun getting old," Mrs. Abbott said. "I guess a lot of people say that shortly before they end up in a place like this." She sighed. "So I'm at Chippiannock. Well, well, well. I'm not sure how I got here, but this is where I wanted to be today." She stared at the couple and said, "Are you here to pay respects to a loved one?"

"Well, um, we . . ." Rudy stammered.

"We came to admire some of the monuments," Connie said.

"You did? How nice. There certainly are some interesting ones. Each stone tells a story. Over yonder, there's a huge anchor partially buried in the ground next to the grave of David Tipton. He was a friend of Mark Twain, don't you know. Tipton was the captain of a snag boat that removed floating debris and logs. Well, anyway, the poor man died of a heart attack while he was at the wheel of his boat on the Mississippi, and his crew honored his life with that anchor.

"Over there, beyond those trees, you'll see an enormous granite sphere on the Robinson family plot. And behind you rests the stone totem pole in honor of Colonel Brian Davenport, a hero of the War of 1812. Did you know he was murdered in his own home?"

Connie and Rudy shook their heads, each wondering if Mrs. Abbott was just making things up or if she really was that knowledgeable.

"I really adore the 'Babyland' section," she continued. "It's sweet but sad seeing the stone monuments of sleeping children. If you help me up, I'll take you to a memorial that means a lot to me. It's just over the knoll." They assisted her as she limped beside the gravestones until the trio came to a life-sized stone sculpture of a Newfoundland dog stretched out on his stomach, his head and paws facing a unique ten-foot-tall monument. On a base that bore the names of Eddie C. and Josie A. stood two red granite pillars connected by a carved stone arch. Each base had the same date: October 22, 1878.

With her cane, Mrs. Abbott gently tapped the head of the dog and said, "Never was there a finer, more loyal companion than Ben." She waddled over to a nearby stone chair carved to look like a tree trunk and sat on it.

She explained that Eddie and Josie were among six

children of Otis and Harriet Dimick. Otis, a wealthy businessman who made his money in real estate and horseracing, and his family lived in a magnificent redbrick mansion on a hill on 21st Avenue overlooking the Mississippi River Valley. Considered a member of the family, Ben the Newfoundland loved all the children, but was especially attached to the two youngest, Josie and Eddie. Ben always accompanied the two to school and would wait outside until recess, when he played with them and their friends. He would linger by the school until class let out and then walk them home.

"I credit that dog with saving my life and Josie's and Eddie's," said Mrs. Abbott. "It happened on Halloween back in 1877. Josie and I were eight and Eddie was four. In those days, we didn't go around knocking on doors and begging for candy on Halloween. We certainly didn't engage in the behavior you see today—soaping windows, egging houses, smashing up pumpkins. None of that. Instead, we dressed up in costumes and went to somebody's house for a Halloween party.

"Well, on this day, we were wearing masks and silly outfits and walking to one of the neighbors for a party. Ben was right by our sides. As we were crossing the street, Eddie found a bracelet that someone had lost. We were standing in the middle of the street examining it. Well, the next block over, a horse pulling a wagon was spooked by something, and he took off without the driver. Ben started barking like mad to alert us, but we didn't pay any attention. The horse turned the corner and was galloping down the street lickety-split right toward us, but we had our backs turned to him. Ben kept barking at us. We turned around and saw that the runaway horse was barreling straight toward us, so we scooted out of the way just in the nick of time. There's no telling what would've happened had Ben not warned us."

"That's quite a story," said Rudy, giving Connie a wink, indicating he didn't believe a word of it.

Connie said to Mrs. Abbott, "You say this happened in 1877. The gravestone says Josie and Eddie died in 1878. They only lived for one more year?"

"Sad but true," Mrs. Abbott replied. "The following October, we were all looking forward to another Halloween party. It was going to be the grandest one of all. Mrs. Dimick and some other wealthy folks—including my parents—were getting together to throw a humdinger with clowns and ponies and a magician. The Dimicks even had a costume for Ben."

But, Mrs. Abbott said, the city was struck by a deadly

outbreak of diphtheria—a highly contagious bacterial disease that causes extreme difficulty breathing and swallowing and often severe damage to the heart and nervous system.

"About two weeks before Halloween, we were at school when Josie and Eddie began having problems breathing," she said. "They were sent home—with Ben by their side of course—on a Friday. By Tuesday, both Josie and Eddie were dead in their home. A disease like that makes no distinction whether you are young or old, rich or poor, good or bad. In this case, it took the lives of two wonderful, innocent children.

"We were all shocked by the news. Mrs. Dimick was so distraught that she couldn't even stand up, and the doctors were worried she would die from grief. It was all she could do to attend the funeral.

"Mr. Dimick knew of Ben's affection for Josie and Eddie, so he let the dog walk behind the hearse. It was drawn by a beautiful horse that brought the bodies here for burial. Every day for about a week afterward, family members visited the graves, and Ben always tagged along. When they stopped their daily visits, Ben took it upon himself to continue coming to this spot. It's about a mile from the Dimicks' house to here, and every morning Ben would walk to the cemetery and stretch out on the gravesite and stay until dark. Then he would return home. This was Ben's routine.

"In the few times that I saw Ben, I could tell he was not his usual self. He had lost his appetite and was getting skinnier. He obviously was mourning the loss of those two precious children. It seemed Ben had a single purpose in life—to guard their graves. This he did with great dedication for about a year until he took his final breath. Everyone said Ben died of a broken heart."

"That is terribly sad," said Connie, brushing away a tear.

"So Ben is buried here under his statue?" Rudy asked.

Mrs. Abbott shook her head and explained, "The Dimicks asked if they could bury Ben next to the children, but the cemetery people refused. So the family buried him on their property. Mr. Dimick was so touched by Ben's devotion to Josie and Eddie that before the dog died he commissioned an artist to sketch the dog here at the graveside. Then he hired a sculptor to create this stone replica.

"I know this might sound silly, but around this time every year, I bring a dog biscuit and place it next to Ben's statue. I've been doing that for years. You know, as a token of my admiration for him. He was an amazing dog." She plucked a dog biscuit out of her purse, handed it to Rudy, and asked, "Would you be so kind?"

After watching him put the treat in front of Ben's statue, she waved to a woman in a white uniform who was about one hundred yards away and hustling toward her. "She looks like someone I should know," Mrs. Abbott said. "Anyway, I want to tell you something else. Ben still looks after children around Halloween. Well, *he* doesn't. His ghost does. He roams between the cemetery and the Dimick house, making sure children in costumes are safe. If they dawdle in the street, he'll shove them to the side. Some youngsters have seen him, and others just feel when he nudges them."

"And you've seen Ben's ghost?" Rudy asked, his eyebrows raised in disbelief.

"Many times," Mrs. Abbott responded. "But that was decades ago. The last time was when I was fifteen and Jimmy Carrington tried to kiss me. Ben growled and scared him off." She smiled and closed her eyes as if exhausted from talking.

Huffing and puffing, the woman in the white uniform arrived. "Oh, lordy, Mrs. Abbott," she gasped. "I've been searching for you for more than an hour. I was worried about you."

Mrs. Abbott opened her eyes and looked somewhat startled. "And you are . . . who?"

"Mrs. Abbott. You know who I am. I'm Mildred; your nurse, remember? You said you were going to take a nap, and then you walked out of the house while I was tending to your medication."

"Medication?" Mrs. Abbott said, looking confused again. "What for?"

Connie took Mildred aside and explained what had happened. The nurse said that Mrs. Abbott was suffering from bouts of senility, adding, "One minute she is perfectly coherent and the next she is, um, shall we say, disoriented."

After the nurse and the old lady left, Connie told Rudy, "I don't think we should be messing around in the cemetery on Halloween. It doesn't seem right. People's sons and daughters and mothers and fathers and grandparents are buried here. This is a place for eternal rest and peace, and we should respect the dead."

"But all the planning we've put into the prank and lining up the college students and everything," Rudy protested. "Connie, you should get your revenge."

"Yes, but not here," she declared. "My mind is made up."

"Okay, then we'll think of another place."

As they walked out of the cemetery, Connie said, "Wasn't that just the most moving story about Ben?"

Rudy rolled his eyes. "Connie, you know how gullible you are."

"Why shouldn't I believe her?"

"Walter—her great-grandson—told me that you can't trust anything she says. Half the time her mind is wandering off someplace in the boondocks."

"But she sounded so sane when she talked about the cemetery and the Dimicks and the dog."

"And the Halloween ghost that growls? Really, Connie? You'll believe anything."

The next afternoon, Connie visited the public library to work on an assignment for history class. She had trouble concentrating on her homework because she couldn't stop thinking about the devoted dog. *I have to check out the story*, she told herself.

She pulled out a thick volume that had bound copies of the local newspaper, the *Rock Island Argus,* for all of 1878. Thumbing through the issue dated October 23, she found this small article:

Sad Bereavement

It becomes our painful duty to report the sad bereavement of the family of O.J. Dimick, Esq., in the death of his two youngest children by diphtheria. Eddie C., a bright boy of five years and two months, and little Josie, as she was familiarly called by her playmates, aged nine years and eight months. Both went to school together on Thursday, both were taken by the terrible disease on Friday, and last night both passed to a better world together and will occupy the same last resting place. Everything that skill and loving attention could do to arrest the disease was without avail, and they now lay side by side in that stricken home, more beautiful than ever, as though the Angel of Death had smiled as he placed his signet upon those childish features.

The funeral will take place tomorrow at 10 A.M.

Wow, what Mrs. Abbott said about the children was true, Connie thought. *But what about the statue of the dog? Did she make that story up?*

Connie examined issues from the 1879 bound works of the *Argus* and came across this article dated August 9:

A Fine Work

O.J. Dimick this morning received a life-size stone image of his Newfoundland dog, which will be placed at the graves of his two children in Chippiannock Cemetery. This dog was greatly attached to the two little ones, whose deaths under such sad circumstances occurred some time ago. He would follow them everywhere, even to school, and when they were taken sick, he still went to the schoolhouse each day, waited patiently for the scholars to come out, and then would make tracks for home alone, looking mournful and anxious. The fidelity of the noble brute was proven on more than one occasion, as the little ones, now dead, were so greatly attached to him. Mr. Dimick determined to have a stone image of the dog made and placed at the graves. Accordingly, he secured the services of a first-class artist in that line of work, Mr. F.O. Coss, of Chicago, and had a sketch drawn of the animal lying down, with head resting on his paws. The contract was given to the Rustic Monument Co., of Chicago, and it is but justice to say that the work is the finest of its kind we have seen. Every feature is clearly defined, the position is natural, while the lifelike expression of the animal classes the work as one of unusual excellence. When the work was finished, it was on exhibition at the warehouse of the Rustic Co., Wabash Avenue, and none passed by without stopping to view the stone image. It is carved out of a solid piece of stone, rustic in finish on the base and displays the work of a master hand in conception and finish. The two little ones at whose graves this additional tribute is placed were wont to romp and play with the reality whose image it is, and when the parents and friends of the two departed visit the graves, that stone image of the noble brute who watched over them in life must bring a reminder of those days which have gone, gone never to return. And there will fall many a silent tear as the beautiful lesson the scene teaches is realized.

Connie had a hard time reading the article because her eyes kept watering up. At school the next day, she told Rudy about the newspaper articles. "Mrs. Abbott was telling the truth all along," Connie declared.

"That's a surprise," Rudy admitted. "But, Connie, a ghost dog looking after children on Halloween? No dice. I'm not buying it."

Connie agreed. "Even for me, that seems just too hard to swallow."

On Halloween night, the pranksters, led by John Bengston and his brother, Brian, walked toward the cemetery with their prey, the innocent Debbie Krueger. Suddenly, two hideous-looking ghouls in tattered clothes and claws for fingers seemingly floated down from the sky directly in front of the Bengstons. Everyone shrieked.

The brothers screamed in voices so high they would have made a choirmaster proud. In the midst of flashes of light, everyone sprinted away, all the while yelling in terror.

From behind a nearby bush where they watched the whole scene unfold, Connie jumped up and down in victory, then hugged Rudy before the two roared with laughter. "It worked to perfection!" she hollered joyously. Calling out to the Augustana College students who took part in the prank, she asked, "Did you get some good pictures?"

"Oh, yeah," said one of the photographers. "You should have seen the looks on the faces of the Bengston brothers."

"You bet," said the other photographer. "Pictures of pure panic."

Connie went over to the "ghouls," hugged them, and gushed, "Thank you so much. You were great!" The two college students in creepy garb had each been in harnesses attached to wires that had been strung over a thick branch of an oak tree. Two members of the college's wrestling team, who had been hiding in the bushes, held the wires while the ghouls were sitting on the branch. When the Bengston group had approached the tree, the ghouls had been lowered in front of them, scaring them silly.

"I can't wait for those photos to get developed," said Connie. "I'm going to plaster them all over the hallways—"

A dog barking furiously interrupted her. They couldn't see the animal, but they could tell it was close and coming from the other side of a hedge by the tree. The dog continued to bark and growl, so everyone backed away. Just then, they heard a loud crack. The branch that the ghouls had been on—the same one that Rudy was standing directly under seconds earlier—suddenly snapped and fell onto the sidewalk with a loud thud.

"Yikes!" Rudy shouted. "That was a close call. We all could have been hurt or killed if it had hit us."

"Thank goodness we moved away when the dog started barking," said Connie. Then she gripped Rudy's arm and pointed down the sidewalk. They both caught a quick glimpse of a large animal before it trotted into the darkness.

"No, it couldn't be," murmured Rudy.

"It sure looked like a dog," Connie said.

"Yeah, like a Newfoundland."

About the Author

Allan Zullo is the author of more than one hundred nonfiction books on subjects ranging from sports and the supernatural to history and animals.

He has written the bestselling Haunted Kids series, published by Scholastic, which is filled with chilling stories based on, or inspired by, documented cases from the files of ghost hunters. Allan also has introduced Scholastic readers to the Ten True Tales series, about people who have met the challenges of dangerous, sometimes life-threatening, situations.

Among his animal-themed books, he has authored *Bad Pets Save Christmas, The Dog Who Saved Christmas and Other True Animal Tales, Christmas Miracle Pets: Animals Who Saved the Day, Bad Pets: True Tales of Misbehaving Pets, Bad Pets on the Loose,* and *Bad Pets Most Wanted.*

Allan, the father of two grown daughters and the grandfather of five, lives with his wife, Kathryn, near Asheville, North Carolina. To learn more about the author, visit his web site at www.allanzullo.com.